THOMAS HOCCLEVE

THOMAS HOCCLEVE

SELECTED POEMS

*edited with an introduction
by Bernard O'Donoghue*

FYFIELD BOOKS
Carcanet   Manchester

Acknowledgements:
I am particularly indebted to the Huntington Library: to its Curator
for sending me microfilms of three manuscripts, HM 111, HM 135
and HM 744, and to the Librarian for kindly giving permission to
quote extensively from them. I should like to thank very much the
staff of the Bodleian Library for a great deal of help, and its keeper
of Western Manuscripts for permission to quote at length from Ms.
Arch. Seld. Supra 53. The Librarian of Durham University Library
kindly allowed me to consult Durham Univ. Cosin V III 9, and
Mr David Burnett gave me useful help and advice with it. I should
like to thank finally for help of various kinds in preparing this
volume Mr Michael Schmidt for his editorial advice, Keith Hanley,
Roger Holdsworth, Catherine La Farge, Desmond O'Brien and my
wife Heather. My greatest general debt is to Professor Norman Davis;
he can be blamed even less than the other people mentioned for the
shortcomings of this volume.

Magdalen College, Oxford

First published in 1982 by
CARCANET NEW PRESS LIMITED
330 Corn Exchange Buildings
Manchester M4 3BG

British Library Cataloguing in Publication Data
    Hoccleve, Thomas
    Selected Poems. — (Fyfield Books)
    I. Title   II. O'Donoghue, Bernard
    821' .2   PR2091

    ISBN 0-85635-321-3

The publisher acknowledges the financial assistance of the
Arts Council of Great Britain

Printed in England by Short Run Press Ltd., Exeter

CONTENTS

Introduction. 7

Thomas Hoccleve's Complaint 19
The Dialogue with a Friend 32
La Male Regle de T. Hoccleve 47
Balade to my Gracious Lord of York. 61
Ad Beatam Virginem 63
To the Duke of Bedford 67
Balade and Rowndel to Somer 68
Three Roundels. 70
The Regement of Princes 73

Notes 100
Bibliography. 103

INTRODUCTION

The reputation of Thomas Hoccleve (c. 1348-1430) has always suffered by association with that of his age. Condemnations of fifteenth-century literature are easy to find: Lounsbury declared the period to have been 'stricken with sterility in every quarter that indicates literary ability of any sort' (*Studies in Chaucer* iii, p. 29); the introduction to the E.E.T.S. *The Pastime of Pleasure* tells us that 'a variety of events conspired to make the time in which (Hawes) was born one of the most uninspiring and depressing in the annals of English poetry' (p.15), and, after commenting on Lydgate's 'interminable verbosity and his habitual prosing', adds that Hoccleve is Lydgate's equal, like him 'only read as a professional duty'. A. R. Myers, giving an account of 'The Arts' in fifteenth-century England, attempts to explain the parallel declines in 'intellectual activity' and in 'courtly verse and art' (*Pelican History of England* 4, p.182).

Few commentators have been generous in their praise of Hoccleve, since William Browne (who says he would have liked to edit more of him) wrote so kindly of him in 1614 at the end of his story of Jonathas, taken from Hoccleve:

> 'Well I wot, the man that first
> Sung this lay, did quench his thirst
> Deeply as did ever one
> In the Muses' Helicon'. (*The Shepherd's Pipe*, Eclogue 1, 749-52)

This is not a common view. From his own century onwards, Hoccleve enjoyed little acclaim, as can be seen from Caroline Spurgeon's *550 Years of Chaucer Criticism and Allusion*, where writer after writer up to the mid-sixteenth-century groups together for praise Chaucer, Gower and Lydgate, often adding to them the names of such writers as Barclay and Hawes, with no mention of Hoccleve. As Lounsbury brutally puts it, 'Occleve is a writer who has been contemptuously treated even by those who speak respectfully of Lydgate'. (p.23)

Nor has Hoccleve's reputation risen greatly since the Elizabethan period. Warton accuses him of a lack of 'invention and fancy', and says that the very 'titles of his pieces indicate a coldness of genius'. Ritson, in 1802, says of Mason's edition (now Huntington 111) that 'six of peculiar stupidity were selected and published by its late owner' (these include the *Male Regle* and the *Somer* poems), and describes the prologue to *The Regement of Princes* as 'sufficiently prolix'. Lounsbury damns Hoccleve with the most backhanded of faint praise, saying that, in spite of the fact that it generally requires 'dogged resolution' to read his works, Hoccleve was morally superior to Lydgate in that he freely admitted that he was dull. He adds: 'most of his poems that have been printed are anything but poetical. The *Letter of Cupid*, found in the folio editions of Chaucer, is tedious beyond description'. (*Studies in Chaucer*, iii, 24).

In Lounsbury's time, as he said, much of Hoccleve had not been printed, and what had been printed was mostly inaccessible. But his name was not cleared by Furnivall's *Early English Texts Society* editions in the 1890's. In the introduction to his edition of the Minor Poems, Furnivall says Hoccleve is deficient both in character and in poetic merit. Evidence for this can be found in the poetry itself (dangerous evidence, one might suppose, in a late medieval poet who was characteristically fond of the mock-modesty formula, and evidence by which Chaucer would not escape whipping): Hoccleve metred amiss, rhymed without skill, got on badly with his wife, was too vain to wear spectacles when he was old, and was, in short, 'a weak, sensitive, look-on-the-worst-side kind of man' (E.E.T.S. 61, p.xxxviii). Furnivall makes no secret of the fact that he found his work on Hoccleve far from compelling. He was easily distracted from it by various projects, such as the great Dictionary, and his endeavours in the scheme of the Hammersmith Girls' Sculling Club, 'for working-girls in shop sewing-rooms, and their brothers and friends, with the after housing of them, and the getting-up Sunday whole-day outings' (E.E.T.S. 72, p. xix). When he took his Hoccleve papers to his holiday farm, he 'never untied the string'. 'Bother Hoccleve! where could he come in, with the sunshine, flowers, apple-orchards and harvest about?' (p. xx). Endearing and sympathetic as is the honesty of this Munbyism and distractability, it did not raise Hoccleve's critical standing.

It is not altogether surprising, then, that the availability of the E.E.T.S. editions did not immediately make Hoccleve popular. C. S. Lewis devotes only one page (though it is a very acute page) of *The Allegory of Love* to Hoccleve: the same as to Barnaby Googe and three fewer than to Nevill. H. S. Bennett, the fifteenth-century's greatest apologist, accords him far from unqualified praise:

> We do not feel that his poems are mechanic exercises, but the reflection of the poet's own ideas and personality. That does not give his verses value, for on the whole Hoccleve has not a sensitive, alert mind. He is an egoist, and the naive outpourings of his own hopes and fears are presented to us in all their crude immediacy. What his mind thought his pen set down without much preliminary attempt to control or refine his matter in a clear picture: yet his dialogue gives the illusion of life: we feel some of the give and take of conversation. . . This immediacy gives what little value may be found in Hoccleve's work. (*Chaucer and the Fifteenth Century.* p.149)

Even this more considered and just account of the poet seems to be on its guard against generosity, carefully qualifying what is praised. Incidental references to Hoccleve are rarely flattering. W. F. Schirmer (in *John Lydgate. A Study in the Culture of the XVth Century* (1952). Trans. A. E. Keep, Methuen 1961) has a low opinion of him, and irritatingly refers to him, indicating manuscript variation, as '(H)occleve' throughout, as if he belonged to a strange, half-capitalising sect. Derek Pearsall (in *John Lydgate*. R.K.P. 1970) resents the fact that literary history assigns to him a place more or less as an equal of Lydgate, because 'on all counts he is a much less important writer' (p. 16).

There is, then, a powerful weight of traditional opinion against Hoccleve. And yet the curious thing is that, at least to the modern taste, he is far from dull. Readers who have approached him with circumspection, often by way of Lydgate, are almost invariably pleasantly surprised. This may well be attributable to a change in literary taste, because Hoccleve's tendency towards autobiographical reminiscence, mentioned by Bennett, is to the modern taste (this

9

accounts, according to Pearsall, for his inflated reputation (p. 17). In any case, while the esteem in which fifteenth-century poetry in general is held has not risen greatly, there have recently been some more enthusiastic appraisals of Hoccleve. The most notable is Jerome Mitchell's 1968 study which describes the content and merit of Hoccleve's writings, though even he rather loses his nerve and ends by claiming that Hoccleve's poetry is 'some of the most readable literature of medieval England' (p. 123). A valuable reassessment is the brief section in Ian Robinson's *Chaucer's Prosody*. The quality that both Mitchell and Robinson emphasise (as had Lewis and Bennett more briefly) is the strikingly personal tone of Hoccleve's writing.

The most valuable service performed by Robinson was to consider Hoccleve on his own, without reference to his supposed dependence on Chaucer and his failure to emulate him. For Furnivall, Hoccleve's 'chief merit is that he was the honourer and pupil of Chaucer'; one of his reasons for choosing Harley 4866 as his source manuscript for *The Regement of Princes* is 'because it has the best portrait of Chaucer'. Miss Hammond (in *English Verse Between Chaucer and Surrey*, p. 56) says 'what recommends Hoccleve to us is his deep and genuine respect for Chaucer'. And ultimately even Robinson does not allow full independence to him; he ends by saying that it was his character, not artistic incompetence, that made him 'unable to occupy the place' after Chaucer, and that he was 'crushed by the load of responsibility' of following the master (p.199). Yet, except in his repeated references to Chaucer, we do not get the impression that Hoccleve is trying to write like Chaucer at all. To adopt Warton's argumentative procedure, the very titles of his most substantial works suggest otherwise. Lydgate's poems constantly suggest Chaucerian influence in their titles, subjects and expression: Hoccleve's very rarely. Pearsall, in his pages on Hoccleve in *Chaucer and Chaucerians* (ed. D. S. Brewer. London 1975; p.222-225), notes that there are far fewer echoes in Hoccleve than in Lydgate. Robinson says that 'Hoccleve does not recognise his real strengths and produces reams of aureate dullness' (*Chaucer's Prosody*, p.212), making the important point that his strength is not in aureate writing. But Hoccleve only uses an aureate style in parts of his short address poems, in his uninspired religious poetry and in his apostrophes to Chaucer:

> 'My mayster Chaucer, flour of eloquence,
> Mirrour of fructuous entendement. . .'
>
> (*The Regement of Princes* 1962-3).

Lydgate's attempts to emulate Chaucer's high style are often disastrously verbose. But it seems hard to accuse Hoccleve of failing to write like Chaucer when it is clear that he mostly wrote in a very different plain style of his own; it is certainly not the whole story, or the most important part of it, to say as Furnivall did that 'the influence of Chaucer is felt all thro Hoccleve' (EETS 61, p. xxxiv).

What, therefore, *is* the the characteristic interest of Hoccleve for the modern reader? Brief quotation will illustrate his lesser virtues. He can arrest the reader's interest, as he does at the opening of his *Dialogue With a Friend*:

> 'And, endid my compleinte in this manere,
> Oon knockid at my chaumbre dore sore
> And criede alowde: 'Howe, Hoccleve, art thou here?
> Open thi dore'.

He can compete with Chaucer and Gower in the felicitous turning of a colloquial phrase. When he was young, he drank except when 'lak of coyn departith conpaignie' (*Male Regle* 133). The power of death over men is succinctly symbolised:

> 'Al that lyf berith with hir chek is maat'.   (*Lerne to Die*, 161)

In translating Christine de Pisan, he often adds vividness to her version:

> 'Mais quant ainsi sont fort envelopées'   (50-1)

becomes

> 'And when the man the pot hath by the stele'   (*Cupide* 50).

But these minor talents are the virtues of the age which a poet of small abilities could learn from the masters Gower and Chaucer.

In Hoccleve they are accompanied by the typical faults of the age, in particular the besetting sin of the fifteenth-century translator, the unenlightening doublet. These are especially rife in Hoccleve's narratives; for instance, in the course of sixteen lines in the story of John of Canace in the *Regement* we find 'opened and unshit' (4243), 'gone and went' (4246) and 'to wite and knowe' (4258). The lapses into aureation mentioned above are another such weakness. But a total judgment cannot be based on such minor talents or foibles.

Hoccleve does have a major virtue; he evokes in an interesting way the circumstances of the unremarkable life of a man in his time, without any inevitable reference to convention or extra-worldly scheme. Perhaps, as G. G. Smith said in *The Transition Period* (Edinburgh 1900; p. 19), the personal element in him is more 'conventional and rhetorical. . . than individual'; Penelope Doob and Eva Thornley (see Bibliography) have both argued interestingly for regarding Hoccleve's madness and his misspent youth as spiritual verisimilitude. As C. S. Lewis says, he is the first writer to describe 'what we call Worry' (*The Allegory of Love*, p. 236):

'Whoso that thoughty is, is wo-bygan'   (*Regement*, 80).

What is remarkable is precisely the lack of any conventional or rhetorical framework. The hardships of the professional writer's life are feelingly described: the pains he develops in his back and stomach and eyes. While workmen talk and sing outside 'in the hottest of all theyr besynes',

'We stope and stare uppon the schepys skynne,
And kepe most our songe and wordys wythyn.'
(*Regement* 1014-15)

The poet's most remarkable achievement of this kind is his description of the distressing aftermath to his nervous breakdown. In his *Complaint* he tells us that he lost his memory but that it was restored five years earlier. But people will not believe him cured, and he has often seen their faces change when they catch sight of him:

'For ofte, whanne I in Westmynstir halle
And eke in Londoun amonge the prees went,
I sy the chere abaten and apalle
Of hem that weren wonte me for to calle
To companie. Her heed they caste awry
Whanne I hem mette, as they not me sy.'   (72-7)

The poet continues that these friends, though they admit that his
raging is now past, still shun him because, as they whisper,

'Resorte it wole, namely in suche age
As he is of'.   (88-9)

The poet goes home, studies a sane expression in the mirror, and tries
to keep that expression so that he will look sane in the street. Then
he thinks that he is perhaps unable to assess the sanity of his appear-
ance if his perception is deranged. The experience is strikingly
evocative of Yeats:

'How in the name of Heaven can he escape
That defiling and disfigured shape
The mirror of malicious eyes
Casts upon his eyes until at last
He thinks that shape must be his shape?'
                              ('A Dialogue of Self and Soul')

Then, one day walking through Westminster, the poet reflects bitterly:

'A greet fool I am
This pavyment a daies thus to bete. . .
Wondringe and hevinesse to purchase,
Sithen I stonde out of al favour and grace'.   (185-6; 188-9)

And, though the medieval poet in Hoccleve is comforted by Reason
and ends by thanking God and casting his sorrow to the cock (386),
it is the distress of the erstwhile madman's avoidance by his friends
that remains with the reader as well as with the poet who returns

to it in the *Dialogue*.

As well as referring to his own problems and failings, Hoccleve's writings are full of allusions to the shortcomings of the times: social foibles, political crookedness and legal chicanery. In the Prologue to the *Regement*, Hoccleve's reverend interlocutor (the habit of referring to him as 'the beggar' is, I think, misleading for his role in the poem) attacks fashionable overdressing, particularly the trend for wearing wide sleeves which wastes cloth and renders servants incapable of helping their masters when they are attacked by restricting their freedom of movement. It was not always so; John of Gaunt's clothes were not too wide. And the section ends, like many another, with an appeal to the country to amend:

> 'O Engelond, stande upright on thy feet!' (537)

There is a complicated description of a con trick played by noblemen's servants on the clerks of the Privy Seal (1499-1533) to avoid paying them, repeated protests at the non-payment of Hoccleve's annuity, and dark hints about the sexual *mores* of the upper orders. There are some attacks on clerical abuses, particularly in connexion with the poet's failure to gain a benefice, but nothing like the vehemence of Langland, Chaucer or *The Plowman's Tale*; he attacks plurality as Chaucer does, but even that is given an economic basis: a parish priest will complain that he cannot *live* on one benefice (*Regement* 1418).

Indeed the kind of clerical complaint made by Hoccleve is one associated with the writers at the turn of the next century, especially Dunbar and Skelton. The section in the *Regement* where he complains at his failure to gain a benefice is inevitably reminiscent of Dunbar's Tungland obsession, open to the same charge of sour grapes. There are other resemblances to these later poets: his concern with the duties of kings and his interest in the city, for instance. He has not, of course, the versatility of Dunbar, nor has he the skill with language and the technical brilliance of that poet and Skelton. But the same variation between the allegorical poems of Dunbar, such as the typically late medieval *The Golden Targe*, and his more modern-seeming personal poems like *The Lament for the Makaris*, or between *The Bouge of Court* and Skelton's more idiosyncratic poems, such as *Speak, Parrot,* is to be seen to some extent in Hoccleve. If the parallels seem slight, their total absence from the more purely medieval poetry of Lydgate shows them to have significance. It is, therefore, surprising to find Alain Renoir in a study of Lydgate describing Hoccleve as 'thoroughly medieval' (*The Poetry of John Lydgate*. RKP 1967, p. 40), though he is doubtless right when he says that in the *Regement* Hoccleve 'devotes so much attention to current events and to his own grievances that he neglects the theoretical aspects of the conduct of rulers which might have appealed to the Renaissance' (p. 136). But the same is true of Dunbar and his contemporaries. Like Dunbar and Henryson, Hoccleve needs to be relieved of the style 'Chaucerian' to be seen for what he is.

I am not, of course, arguing that Hoccleve was the founder of a school of poetry that came to fruition in Dunbar or Skelton. Indeed, while stressing that he does not belong in the allegorical tradition of Chaucer, it is clear that Hoccleve's chosen subjects belong firmly in the medieval tradition which Gower represents in English. Hoccleve often evokes the major themes of Gower's works in his major works, particularly in his political concern with good government and the ordering of society. J. H. Fisher (in *John Gower: Moral Philosopher and Friend of Chaucer*. London 1965) draws attention to the parallel views on kingship of the two poets, and might have considered their affinities further. For instance the form and terminology of the confessional exchanges between Amans and the Confessor of the *Confessio Amantis* are paralleled often in Hoccleve: the old man in the *Regement* prologue calls Hoccleve 'sone myn' and is addressed as 'fadir'; in the poems of the linked *Series*, the old man's didactic and discussing role is taken by the friend; and in *Lerne to Die*, the disciple's exchanges are with the image of the dying man and with Sapience. Practically all of Hoccleve's writing has the intention of instructing as well as diverting that Gower declares in the *Confessio*.

But to over-emphasise his debt to Gower or to Chaucer, or to see him as anticipating Dunbar, is less valuable than to appreciate Hoccleve in his own terms. If he is not especially original, he is at least unique as a fifteenth-century poet. He is the earliest and inchoate exponent of a mixed kind of writing that is found up to the early Elizabethans: neither thoroughly medieval nor satisfying to the curiosity of the Renaissance, drawing on conventional frameworks and apparently real experiences at the same time. In wit and moral content much of what the later writers in that minor tradition have to offer surpasses the modest *oeuvre* of Hoccleve; but few of them equal him in the biographical interest of the incidental details that he gives of his unspectacular life.

Most discussion of Hoccleve's language and style has centred on his metre, rightly, because it was the belief that his metre was incompetent that led so many commentators from the sixteenth century onwards to dismiss him. (Mitchell's discussion of other aspects of his language—diction, syntax and rhetoric—seems judicious and persuasive, although extended literary consideration remains to be made.)

The comments on his metre have followed the pattern of the debate on Chaucer's metre, but in an extreme form. A. H. Licklider (*Chapters on the Metric of the Chaucerian Tradition*. Baltimore 1910) gives Hoccleve as the chief exponent of thwarted stress. Furnivall says 'so long as he can count ten syllables by his fingers, he is content' (EETS 61, p. xli), and Saintsbury says 'the whole thing is prosaic, hobbling, broken-backed doggerel' (*History of English Prosody* 1906; I, 234). Miss Hammond says he is 'metrically incompetent' (p. 55), and even C. S. Lewis, in his more enlightened proposal of the 'fifteenth-century heroic line' as an answer to the scansion problems of the poetry of the period, admits that 'most of Hoccleve will not fit in at all' (*Essays and Studies*, 1938; p. 37). The most recent champion of reading Chaucerian poetry as strict iambic pentameter understandably does not mention Hoccleve at all (P. F. Baum, *Chaucer's Verse*. Duke U.P. 1961).

The more impressionistic school of metrical critics are less unkind to Hoccleve, though Southworth makes a cryptic criticism: '(Hoccleve) had caught the surface rhythms of Chaucer's verse but did not have within himself the ability to feel them deeply, and incidentally, to modify them to his own inner needs' (*Verses of Cadence. An Introduction to the Prosody of Chaucer and his Followers*. p.78, Blackwell,

Oxford 1954). Ian Robinson feels that Hoccleve is *too* adept an exponent of what he calls Chaucer's 'balanced pentameter', 'being too much of a metrical specialist' (p.193). He adds that 'the deliberate preference for the laboured and artificial is very typical of the earlier Chaucerians'. Mitchell's detailed analysis of the metre concludes that 'there is no thwarted stress in Hoccleve' (p. 109).

There is no doubt that Hoccleve's metre is difficult to read for the modern reader, whether or not the explanation is an excess rather than a deficiency in competence. The reader who is distracted by the apparent roughness of the metre is recommended to consult Mitchell and Robinson. Here I shall give only a single example to suggest why Hoccleve seems not to be failed iambic pentameter. Furnivall amends line 31 of the *Regement* from

> 'For she knewe no lowere discension',

to

> 'For that she knewe no lowere discension',

supplying a 'that' which is found in none of the manuscripts to make the metre, as Furnivall saw it, correct. But surely, to use a simplified version of Robinson's argument, if such a simple stratagem would make a wrong metrical line right, the poet himself or one of the early scribes (who adapted very freely) would have adopted it. It is better to revise our definition of correctness in the metre, which can perhaps only be deduced from the text anyway.

In selecting the texts to edit, I have drawn heavily on the 'auto-biographical' passages because they are the most interesting to us and the most typical of what is unusual in Hoccleve. I have included whole poems or long excerpts as often as possible; it is because of this that the *Epistle of Cupid*, some of Hoccleve's most elegant and masterly writing, is not represented, to my regret. I have retained the orthography of the manuscripts, except in the following instances: words divided in the manuscripts ('un to') I have joined in keeping with the modern practice ('unto') for ease of reading; ampersands are expanded to 'and'; u/v and i/j positional variants are modernised; where the manuscripts have *yogh* and *thorn* I have invariably written 'gh' and 'th'; I have dispensed occasionally with a few random

17

capitals ('joy' for 'Joy'); and I have attempted to give helpful modern punctuation throughout. I have not altered final 'e's' or anything that affects scansion. I am very aware that there are two spelling systems in the manuscripts: that of HM 135 ('schall', etc.) and that of the Arch Selden manuscript. But, before the findings of the work now being done on Hoccleve manuscripts, any attempt to reach the poet's original spelling would be hopeless.

THOMAS HOCCLEVE'S COMPLAINT

*Edited from Ms. Arch. Seld. Supra 53, compared with the Stowe text
of Ms. Durham Cosin V iii 9.*

Aftir that hervest inned had hise sheves,   autumn had harvested
And that the broun sesoun of mihelmesse
Was come and gan the trees robbe of her leves
That grene hed ben and in lusty freisshenesse,
And hem into colour of yelownesse   (5)
Had died and doun throwen undir foote,   dyed
That chaunge sanke into myn herte roote.

For freisshly broughte it to my remembraunce
That stablenesse in this worlde is ther noon.
Ther is no thing but chaunge and variaunce.   (10)
Howe welthi a man be, or wel be goon,   however; well provided
Endure it shal not: he shal it forgoon.   lose
Deeth undir foote shal him thriste adoun;
That is every wightes conclucioun,

Wiche for to weyve is in no mannes myght,   avoid
Howe riche he be, stronge, lusty, freissh and gay.   (16)
And in the ende of Novembre, uppon a night,
Sighynge sore as I in my bed lay
For this and othir thoughtis wiche many a day   (19)
Byforne I tooke, sleep cam noon in myn ye,   took heed of
So vexid me the thoughtful maladie.   worrying

I sy wel, sithin I with siknesse last   saw; since
Was scourgid, cloudy hath bene the favour
That shoon on me ful bright in times past.
The sunne abated, and the dirke shour   (25)
Hilded doun right on me, and in langour   poured
Me made swymme, so that my spirite
To lyve no lust had ne no delite.

The greef aboute myn herte so sore swal   (29)
And bolned evere to and to so sore   swelled

That nedis oute I muste ther withal.
I thoughte I nolde kepe it cloos no more,
Ne lete it in me for to eelde and hore.   to age; grow grey
And, for to preve I cam of a womman,   (34)
I braste oute on the morwe and thus bigan.   burst out next day

Here endith my prolog: and folwith my compleinte.

Almyghty god, as liketh his goodnesse,   pleases
Vesiteth Folke al day, as men may se,
With los of good and bodily sikenesse.
And amonge othir he forgat not me.
Witnesse uppon the wilde infirmite   (40)
Wiche that I hadde, as many a man wel knewe,
And wiche me oute of my silfe caste and threwe.

It was so knowen to the peple and kouthe   known
That counseil was it noon, ne not be might.   secret
Howe it with me stood was in every mannes mouthe,   (45)
And that ful sore my frendis affright.
They for myn helthe pilgrimages hight   promised
And soughte hem, somme on hors and somme on foote,
(God yelde it hem!) to gete me my boote.   cure

But although the substaunce of my memorie   (50)
Wente to pleie, as for a certein space,   went off duty
Yit the lorde of vertue, the kyng of glorie,
Of his highe myght and his benigne grace,
Made it for to retourne into the place
Whens it cam; wiche at alle halwemesse   All Saints' (1 Nov.)
Was five yeere, neither more ne lesse.   (56)

And evere sithin (thankid be god oure lord
Of his good and gracious reconsiliacioun),
My wit and I have bene of suche acord
As we were or the alteracioun   before
Of it was. But, by my savacioun,   (61)

20

Sith that time have I be sore sette on fire
And lyved in greet turment and martire.

For, though that my wit were hoom come agein,
Men wolde it not so undirstonde or take.   (65)
With me to dele hadden they disdein.
A rietous persone I was, and forsake.   dissolute; abandoned
Min oolde frendshipe was al overshake;   passed away
No wight with me list make daliaunce.   conversation
The worlde me made a straunge countinuaunce.   (70)

With that myn herte sore gan to tourment.
For ofte, whanne I in Westmynstir halle
And eke in Londoun amonge the prees went,
I sy the chere abaten and apalle   saw; grow dim
Of hem that weren wonte me for to calle   (75)
To companie. Her heed they caste awry
Whanne I hem mette, as they not me sy.

As seide is in the sauter might I sey: Psalms
They that me sy fledden awey fro me.
Forgeten I was, all oute of mynde awey,   (80)
As he that deed was from hertis cherte.   affection
To a lost vessel lickned mighte I be;
For manie a wight aboute me dwelling
Herde I me blame and putte in dispreisyng.

Thus spake manie oone and seide by me: (85)
'Although from him his syknesse savage
Withdrawen and passed, as for a time, be,
Resorte it wole, namely in suche age
As he is of.' And thanne my visage
Bigan to glowe for the woo and fere.   (90)
Tho wordis, hem unwar, cam to myn eere.   those; unknown

'Whanne passinge hete is,' quod thei, 'trustith this:
Assaile him wole agein that maladie.'

21

And yit, parde, thei token hem amis.
Noon effecte at al took her prophecie. (95)
Manie someris bene past sithen remedie
Of that god of his grace me purveide. provided
Thankid be god, it shoop not as thei seide.

What falle shal, what men so deme or gesse, befall
To him that woot every hertis secree (100)
Reserved is. It is a lewidnesse folly
Men wiser hem pretende than thei be.
And no wight knowith, be it he or she,
Whom, howe ne whanne god wole him vesite.
It happith often whanne men wene it lite. (105)

Somtime I wende as lite as any man expected
For to han falle into that wildenesse.
Bot god, whanne him liste, may, wole and can
Helthe withdrawe and sende a wight syknesse.
Though man be wel this day, no sikernesse (110)
To hym bihighte is that it shal endure.
God hurte nowe can, and nowe hele and cure.

He suffrith longe, but at the laste he smit. tolerates
Whanne that a man is in prosperite,
To drede a falle comynge it is a wit. sensible
Whoso that taketh hede ofte may se (116)
This worldis chaunge and mutabilite
In sondry wise, howe nedith not expresse.
To my mater streite wole I me dresse.

Men seiden I loked as a wilde steer, (120)
And so my looke aboute I gan to throwe.
Min heed to hie, anothir seide, I beer:
'Ful bukkissh is his brayn, wel may I trowe.'
And seide the thridde (and apt is in the rowe
To site of hem that a resounles reed (125)
Can geve): 'no sadnesse is in his heed.' stability

22

Chaunged had I my pas, somme seiden eke,
For here and there forthe stirte I as a roo: capered
Noon abood, noon areest, but al brainseke.
Another spake and of me seide also,   (130)
My feet weren ay wavynge to and fro
Whanne that I stonde shulde and with men talke,
And that myn yen soughten every halke.

I leide an eere ay to, as I by wente,   (134)
And herde al, and thus in myn herte I caste: uttered
'Of longe abidinge here I may me repente.
Lest that of hastinesse I at the laste
Answere amys, beste is hens hie faste.
For if I in this prees amys me gye,   'guy': i.e. conduct
To harme wole it me turne and to folie.'   (140)

And this I demed wel and knewe wel eke:
What so that evere I shulde answere or seie,
They wolden not han holde it worth a leke.
For why, as I had lost my tunges keie   therefore
Kepte I me cloos, and trussid me my weie,   took myself off
Droupinge and hevy and al woo bistaad.   beset
Smal cause hadde I, me thoughte, to be glad.   (147)

My spirites labouriden evere ful bisily
To peinte countenaunce, chere and look,
For that men spake of me so wondringly,   (150)
And for the verry shame and feer I qwook.   quaked
Though myn herte hadde be dippid in the brook,
It weet and moist was ynow of my swoot,
Wiche was nowe frosty colde, nowe firy hoot.

And in my chaumbre at home whanne that I was,   (155)
My silfe aloone, I in this wise wrought:
I streite unto my mirrour and my glas
To loke howe that me of my chere thought,
If any othir were it than it ought.

For fain wolde I, if it not had bene right,   (160)
Amendid it to my kunnynge and myght.

Many a saute made I to this mirrour,   attack
Thinking: 'if that I looke in this manere
Amonge folke as I nowe do, noon errour
Of suspecte look may in my face appere.   (165)
This countinaunce, I am sure, and this chere,
If I it forthe use, is no thing reprevable   from now on
To hem that han conceitis resonable.'

And ther with al, I thoughte thus anoon:
'Men in her owne cas bene blinde alday,   (170)
As I have herde seie manie a day a goon,
And in that same plite I stonde may.
Howe shal I do? Wiche is the beste way
My troublid spirit for to bringe in rest?
If I wiste howe, fain wolde I do the best.'   (175)

Sithen I recovered was, have I ful ofte   since
Cause had of anger and inpacience,
Where I borne have it esily and softe,
Suffringe wronge be done to me and offence
And not answerid agen but kepte seilence,   (180)
Leste that men of me deme wolde and sein,
'Se howe this man is fallen in agein.'   relapsed

As that I oones fro Westminstir cam,
Vexid ful grevously with thoughtful hete,
Thus thoughte I: 'A greet fool I am   (185)
This pavyment a daies thus to bete,
And in and oute laboure faste and swete,
Wondringe and hevinesse to purchace,
Sithen I stonde out of al favour and grace.'

And thanne thoughte I, on that othir side: (190)
'If that I not be sen amonge the prees,

24

Men deme wole that I myn heed hide
And am werse than I am, it is no lees.'   lies
O lorde, so my spirit was restelees,
I soughte reste and I not it fonde,   (195)
But ay was trouble redy at myn honde.

I may not lette a man to ymagine   prevent
Fer above the mone, if that him liste.
Therby the sothe he may not determine,
But by the preef ben thingis knowen and wiste.   (200)
Many a doom is wrappid in the myste.   fate
Man bi hise dedis, and not by hise lookes,
Shal knowen be, as it is writen in bookes.

Bi taaste of fruit men may wel wite and knowe   know
What that it is. Othir preef is ther noon.   (205)
Every man woote wel that, as that I trowe.
Right so, thei that deemen my wit is goon
(As yit this day ther deemeth many oon
I am not wel) may, as I by hem goo,   (209)
Taaste amd assay if it be so or noo.   test, try

Uppon a look is harde men hem to grounde   form an opinion
What a man is. Therby the sothe is hid.
Whethir hise wittis seek bene or sounde,
By countynaunce is it not wist ne kid.
Though a man harde have oones ben bitid,   befallen
God shilde it shulde on him contynue alway.   (216)
By communynge is the beste assay.   talking

I mene, to commune of thingis mene,   insignificant
For I am but right lewide douteles   unlearned
And ignoraunt; my kunnynge is ful lene.   (220)
Yit homely resoun knowe I neverethelees.
Not hope I founden be so resounlees
As men deemen: Marie, crist forbede!
I can no more. Preve may the dede.

25

If a man oones falle in drunkenesse,   (225)
Shal he contynue therynne evere mo?
Nay! Though a man do in drinking excesse
So ferforthe, that not speke he ne can, ne goo,   extremely
And hise wittis welny bene refte him fro
And buried in the cuppe, he aftirward   (230)
Cometh to hym silfe agein; ellis were it hard.

Right so, though that my witte were a pilgrim
And wente fer from home, he cam again.
God me devoided of the grevous venim
That had enfectid and wildid my brain.   (235)
See howe the curteise leche moost soverain   physician
Unto the seke geveth medicine
In nede, and hym releveth of his grevous pine.

Nowe lat this passe; god woot, many a man
Semeth ful wys by countenaunce and chere,   (240)
Wiche, and he tastid were what he can,   tested
Men mighten licken him to a fooles peere.
And somman loketh in foltisshe manere,   foolish
As to the outwarde doom and jugement,
That at the preef discreet is and prudent.   (245)

But algatis, howe so be my countinaunce,   anyway
Debaat is nowe noon bitwixe me and my wit,   dissencion
All though that ther were a disseveraunce,
As for a time, bitwixe me and it.
The gretter harme is myn, that nevere yit   (250)
Was I wel lettrid, prudent and discreet.
Ther nevere stood yit wys man on my feet.

The sothe is this: suche conceit as I had
And undirstonding, al were it but smal,
Bifore that my wittis weren unsad,   unstable
Thanked be oure lorde Ihesu crist of al,   (256)
Suche have I nowe. But blowe is ny overal   said

26

The reverse, wherthorugh moche is my mornynge,
Wiche causeth me thus syghe in compleinynge.

Sithen my good fortune hath chaungid hir chere,   (260)
Hie tyme is me to crepe into my grave.
To lyve joielees, what do I here?
I in myn herte can no gladnesse have.
I may but smal seie, but if men deme I rave.   without men thinking
Sithen othir thing than woo may I noon gripe,   (265)
Unto my sepulcre am I nowe ripe.

My wele, a dieu! farwel, my good fortune!
Oute of youre tables me planed han ye.   writing-tablets; erased
Sithen welny eny wight for to commune
With me loth is, farwel prosperite!   (270)
I am no lenger of youre livere.
Ye have me putte oute of youre retenaunce.   retinue
A dieu, my good aventure and good chaunce!

And aswithe aftir, thus bithoughte I me: immediately
'If that I in this wise me dispeire,   (275)
It is purchas of more adversite.
What nedith it my feble wit appeire?   impair
Sith god hath made myn helthe home repeire,
Blessid be he! And what men deme and speke,   (279)
Suffre it thenke I, and me not on me wreke.   punish

But somdel had I rejoisinge amonge   a little
And a gladnesse also in my spirite,
That, though the peple took hem mis and wronge
Me deemyng of my syknesse not quite,
Yit, for they compleined the hevy plite   (285)
That they had seen me in, with tendirnesse
Of hertis cherte, my greef was the lesse.

In hem putte I no defaute but oon:
That I was hool thei not ne deme kowde,

And day by day thei sye me bi hem goon   (290)
In hete and coolde, and neither stille or lowde
Knewe thei me do suspectly. A dirke clowde
Hir sight obscurid, withynne and withoute,
And for al that were ay in suche a doute.   just because of that

Axide han they ful ofte sithe and freined   inquired
Of my felawis of the prive seel,   (296)
And preied hem to telle hem with herte unfeined
Howe it stood with me, wethir yvel or wel.
And they the sothe tolde hem everydel;
But thei helden her wordis not but lees.   lies
Thei mighten as wel have holden her pees.   (301)

This troubly lyf hath al to longe endurid.
Not have I wist hou in my skyn to tourne.
But nowe my silfe to my silfe have ensurid   pledged
For no suche wondringe aftir this to mourne.   (305)
As longe as my lyf shal in me sojourne,
Of suche ymaginynge I not me recche.
Lat hem deeme as hem list, and speke and drecche.   fantasise

This othir day, a lamentacioun
Of a wooful man in a book I sy,   (310)
To whom wordis of consolacioun
Resoun gaf, spekynge effectuelly.
And wel esid myn herte was therby,
For whanne I had a while in the book reed,   (314)
With the speche of resoun was I wel feed.   paid

The hevy man, wooful and angwisshous,   anguished
Compleined in this wise, and thus seide he:
'My lyf is unto me ful encomborus.
For whidre or unto what place I flee,
My wickidnessis evere folowen me,   (320)
As men may se the shadwe a body sue;   pursue
And in no manere I may hem eschewe.

28

'Vexacioun of spirit and turment
Lacke I right noon. I have of hem plente.
Wondirly bittir is my taast and sent.   (325)
Woo be the time of my nativite,
Unhappi man, that evere shulde I be!
O deeth, thi strook a salve is of swetnesse
To hem that lyven in suche wrecchidnesse.

'Gretter plesaunce were it me to die,   (330)
By manie foolde, than for to lyve so.
Sorwes so manie in me multiplie
That my lyf is to me a verre foo.
Comforted may I not be of my woo.
Of my distresse see noon ende I can.   (335)
No force howe soone I stinte to be a man.'   it doesn't matter

Thanne spake Resoun: 'What meneth al this fare?
Though welthe be not frendly to thee yit,
Oute of thin herte voide woo and care.'
'By what skile, howe, and by what reed and wit',   (340)
Seide this wooful man, 'mighte I doon it?'
'Wrastle', quod Resoun, 'agein hevynesse
Of the worlde: troublis, suffringe and duresses.

'Biholde howe many a man suffrith dissese
As greet as thou—and al away grettere;   (345)
And though it hem pinche sharply and sese,
Yit paciently thei it suffre and bere.
Thinke hereon, and the less it shal the dere.   harm
Suche suffraunce is of mannes gilte clensinge,
And hem enableth to joye everelastinge.   (350)

'Woo, hevinesse and tribulacioun
Comen aren to men alle, and profitable.
Though grevous be mannes temptacioun,
It sleeth man not to hem that ben suffrable   patient
And to whom goddis strook is acceptable.   (355)

29

Purveied joie is, for god woundith tho   *foreseen*
That he ordeined hath to blis to goo.

'Golde purgid is, thou seest, in the furneis
For the finer and clenner it shal be.   (359)
Of thi dissese the weighte and the peis   *weight*
Bere lightly. For god, to prove the,   *because*
Scourgid the hath with sharpe adversite,
Not grucche and seie, "whi susteine I this?".   *do not*
For, if thou do, thou the takist amis.

'But thus thow shuldist thinke in thin herte   (365)
And seie: "To thee, lorde god, I have agilte   *offended*
So sore, I moot, for myn offensis, smerte
As I am worthi. O lorde, I am spilte   *deserve*
But thou to me thi mercy graunte wilte.
I am ful sure; thou maist it not denie.   (370)
Lorde, I me repente, and I the mercy crie".'

Lenger I thoughte reed have in this book,
But so it shope that I ne mighte naught.   *happened*
He that it oughte agen it to him took,   *owned*
Me of his hast unwar. Yit have I caught   (375)
Sum of the doctrine by resoun taught
To the man, as above have I said,
Whereof I holde me ful wel apaid.

For evere sithen, sett have I the lesse
By the peples ymaginacioun,   (380)
Talkinge this and that of my siknesse
Wich cam of goddis visitacioun
Mighte I have be founde in probacioun
Not grucching, but han take it in souffraunce,
Holsum and wys had be my governaunce.   (385)

Farwel, my sorowe! I caste it to the cok.
With pacience I hensforthe thinke unpike

30

Of suche thoughtful dissese and woo the lok
And lete hem out, that han me made to sike.   sigh
Hereafter oure lorde god may, if him like,   (390)
Make al myn oolde affeccioun resorte.
And in hope of that wole I me comforte.   confidence

Thorugh goddis just doom and his jugement,
And for my best, nowe I take and deem,   good
Gaf that good lorde me my punischement.   (395)
In welthe, I tooke of him noon hede or yeme   care
Him for to plese and him honoure and queme;   please
And he me gaf a boon on for to gnawe,
Me to correcte and of him to have awe.

He gaf me wit, and he tooke it away   (400)
Whanne that he sy that I it mis dispente,
And gaf agein whanne it was to his pay.   pleasure
He grauntide me my giltis to repente,
And hensforwarde to sette myn entente
Unto his deitee to do plesaunce,   (405)
And to amende my sinful governaunce.

Laude and honour and thanke unto thee be,
Lorde god that salve art to al hevinesse.
Thanke of my welthe and myn adversitee,
Thanke of myn elde and of my seeknesse.   (410)
And thanke be to thin infinit goodnesse,
For thi giftis and benefices alle;   blessings
And unto thi mercy and grace I calle.

THE DIALOGUE WITH A FRIEND

Edited from Ms. Arch. Selden Supra 53, compared with Durham Ms.
Cosin. V iii 9 from line 253; before that with the Durham Stowe
transcript.

And, endid my compleinte in this manere,
Oon knockid at my chaumbre dore sore
And criede alowde: 'Howe, Hoccleve, art thou here?
Open thi dore. Me thinketh ful yore
Sithen I the sy. What, man, for goddis ore,   saw, mercy
Come oute; for this quarter I not the sy,   (6)
By ought I woote.' And oute to hym cam I.

This man was my good frende of fern agoon
That I speke of. And thus he to me seide:
'Thomas, as thou me lovest, telle anoon: (10)
What didist thou whanne I knockede and leide
So faste uppon thi dore?' And I obeide
Unto his wil. 'Come in,' quod I, 'and see.'
And so he dide; he streit wente in with me.   (14)

To my good frende not thoughte I to make it queinte,   to behave
Ne my labour from him to hide or leine,   'lain', to hide [deceitfully
And right anoon I redde hym my compleinte.
And, that done, thus he seide: 'Sinn we tweine
Ben here and no mo folke, for goddis peine,
Thomas, suffre me speke and be not wrooth,   (20)
For the to offende were me ful looth.

'That I shal seie shal be of good entente.
Hast thow maad this compleint forth to goo
Amonge the peple?' 'Ye, frende; so I mente.
What ellis?' 'Nay, Thomas, war! Do not so.   (25)
If thou be wys of that mater, ho.   stop
Reherse thou it not ne it awake.
Kepe al that cloos, for thin honours sake.

'Howe it stood with thee leide is al aslepe.
Men han forgete it; it is oute of mynde. (30)
That thou touche therof I not ne kepe. like
Lat be; that reede I, for I can not finde
O man to speke of it. In as good a kinde
As thou hast stonde amonge men or this day
Stondist thou nowe.' 'A, nay,' quod I, 'nay, nay! (35)

'Though I be lewide, I not so ferforthe dote. stupid
I woote what men han seide and seien of me.
Her wordis have I not as yit forgote.
But greet mervaile have I of yow, that ye
No bet of my compleint avisid be, (40)
Sithen, mafey, I not redde it unto you
So longe agoon, for it was but right now.

'If ye took hede, it maketh mencioun
That men of me speke in myn audience
Ful hevily. Of youre entencioun (45)
I thanke you, for of benevolence,
Woote I ful wel, procedeth youre sentence. opinion
But certis, good frende, that thing that I heere
Can I witnesse and unto it refeere. assign to its origin

'And, whereas that ye me counseile and rede when
That for myn honour shulde I by no weie (51)
Any thing mynge or touche of my wildhede, recall
I unto that answere thus and seie:
Of goddis strook, howe so it peise or weie,
Ought no man to thinke repreef or shame. (55)
His chastisinge hurtith no mannes name.

'Anothir thing ther meveth me also:
Sithen my seeknesse sprad was so wide
That men knewe wel howe it stood with me tho,
So wolde I nowe, uppon that othir side, (60)
Wist were howe oure lorde ihesu, wich is gide

To al releef and may alle hertis cure,
Releved hath me, sinful creature.

'Had I be for an homicide iknowe,
  Or an extorcioner or a robbour,   (65)
Or for a coin clipper as wyde yblowe   *reputed*
  As was my seeknesse; or a werriour
Agein the feith, or a false maintenour   *prosecutor of a legal action*
  Of causes: though I had amendid me,
Hem to han mynged had ben nicite.   *recalled, folly*

'And whi: for tho proceden of freelte   (71)
  Of man hym silfe; he brewith alle tho.
For, sithen god to man yove hath liberte   *given*
  Wiche chese may for to do wel or no,
  If he myschese, he is his owene foo.   *choose wrong*
And to reherse his gilte wich him accusith   (76)
  Honour seith nay; there he scilence excusith.

'But this is al another caas sothly.
  This was the strook of god; he yaf me this.
And sithen he hath withdrawe it curteisly,   (80)
  Am I not holden tell it out? O yis!   *obliged*
But if god had this thanke, it were amis.   *unless*
  In feith, frende, make I thenke an open shrifte   *I intend to make*
  And hide not what I had of his gifte.

'If that a leeche curid had me so   (85)
  (As they lacken alle that science and might),
A name he shulde han had for evere mo,
  What cure he had doon to so seek a wight.
  And yit my purs he wolde have made ful light.
But curteis ihesu, of his grace pacient,   (90)
  Axith not but of gilte amendement.

'The benefice of God not hid be sholde.
  Sithen of myn heele he gaf me the triacle,   *cure*

34

It to confesse and thanke hym am I holde
For he in me hath shewid his miracle.   (95)
His visitacioun is a spectacle   means of seeing
In wiche that I biholde may and se
Bet than I dide howe greet a lord is he.

'But, freend, amonge the vicis that right now
Rehercid I, oone of hem, dar I seie,   (100)
Hath hurte me sore (and I woote wel ynow
So hath it mo) wiche is feble moneie.   underweight
Manie a man this day, but thei golde weie,
Of men not wole it take ne resceive;
And, if it lacke his peis, thei wole it weive.   weight, refuse

'How may it holde his peis, whanne it is wasshe   (106)
So that it lacke sumwhat in thiknesse?
The false peple nothing hem abaisshe;
To clippe it eke in brede and roundenesse
Is that it shulde be alweie the lesse.   (110)
The pore man, amonge alle othir, is
Ful sore anoied and greved in this.

'If it be golde, and hool, that men him profre
For his laboure or his chaffre lent,   merchandise
Take it if him list, and putte it in his cofre.   (115)
For waisshinge or clipping, holde him content
Or leve, he gete noon othir paiement.
It semeth but smal othir is ther.
Trouthe is absent, but falsheed is not fer.

'Howe shal the pore do if in his holde   (120)
No more moneie he ne have at al,
Parcas, but a noble or halpenie of golde,
And it so thynne is and so narowe and smal
That men the eschaunge eschewen overal?   (124)
Not wil it goo, but miche he theronne lesse.   much; lose
He moot do so; he may noon other chese.   choose

35

'I my silfe in this caas ben have or this,   before
Wherfore I knowe it a greet dele the bet.
He that in falsing of coyn gilty is   (129)
Hath greet wronge that he nere on the gebet.   gallows
It is pitee that he therfrom is let,   prevented
Sithen he therto hath so greet title and right.
Regne, justice, and preve on him thi myght.'

(Lines 134-196: Hoccleve continues his attack on these anti-
social coin-clippers and counterfeiters, fearing that they have the
cunning to escape their rightful punishment.)

'Lo, frende, nowe have I myn entent unreke,   revealed
Of my longe tale displese yow nought.'
'Nay, Thomas, nay. But lat me to the speke:
Whanne thi compleinte was to the ende ybrought,   (200)
Cam it ought in thi purpos and thi thought
Ought ellis therwith to han maad than that?'
'Yee, certein, frende.' 'O nowe, good Thomas, what?'

'Frende, that I shal telle as blyve, ywys.
In latyn have I seen a smal tretice   (205)
Wiche "Lerne for to die" called is.
A bettir restreint knowe I noon fro vice;
For whanne that deeth shal man fro hennes trice,   snatch
But he that lessoun lerned have or thanne,   (209)
War that for deeth cometh: woot there no wight whanne.'   beware
                                                    [of the fact that

(211-238: Hoccleve says he intends to translate *Lerne to Die*
to encourage men to repent of their sins before their death, and
that he has been urged to this project by the 'monicion of a
devout man'.)

'And, whanne that endid is, I nevere thinke
More in englissh aftar be occupied.   (240)
I may not labour as I dide and swinke.

Mi lust is not therto so wel applied
As it hath ben; it is ny mortified.
Wherfore I cesse thinke, be this doon.   *intend to stop*
The night approcheth; it is fer past noon.   (245)

'Of age am I fifty wintir and three.
Ripenesse of deeth faste uppon me now hastith.
My lymes sumdel now unweldy be;
Also my sight appeirith faste and wastith,
And my conceit adaies nowe not tastith   *mental capacities*
As it hath doon in yeeris precedent.   (251)
Nowe al another is my sentement.   *feelings*

'More am I hevy nowe uppon a day
Than I somtime was in daies five.
Thing that or this me thought game and play   (255)
Is ernest nowe. The hony from the hive
Of my spirit withdrawith wonder blyve.
Whanne al is doon, this worldis swetnesse
At ende turneth into bitternesse.

'The fool, thorugh love of this lyf present,   (260)
Disceived is; but the wys man woot wel
Howe ful this worlde of sorwe is and torment,
Wherfore in it he trustith not a del.
Though a man this day sitte highe on the wheel,
Tomorwe he may be triced from his sete.   *snatched*
This hath be seen ofte amonge the grete.   (266)

'Howe faire thing, or howe precious it be   *however*
That in the worlde is, it is like a flour
To whom nature yoven hath beaute
Of fresshe hewe and of ful plesant colour,   (270)
With swoot smellyng, also, and odour.
But as soone as that it bicome is drie,
Farwell, colour! and the smel gynneth die.

'Rial myght and al erthely majestee,
Welthe of the worlde, and longe and faire daies   (275)
Passen as dooth the shadowe of a tree.
Whanne deeth is come there bene no delaies.
The worldis trust is brotil at assaies.   brittle
The wise men wel knowen that this is soth;
Thei knowen what disceit to man it dooth.   (280)

'Land, rente, catel, gold, honour and ricchesse   goods
That for a tyme ben lente us to ben ouris
Forgo we shal sonner than we gesse.
Paleis, maneris, castels grete and touris
Shul us birefte be by deeth that ful sour is.   (285)
She is the rowgh besom wiche shal us alle   broom
Swepe out of this worlde, whanne god list it falle.

'And sithen that she shal of us make an ende,
Holsom it is here have ofte in remembraunce,   her
Or she hir messager seeknesse us sende.   (290)
Now, my freend, so god geve yow good chaunce,
Is it not good to make a purviaunce
Agein the comynge of that messagere,
That we may stonde in conscience clere?'

'Yis, Thomas yis; thou hast a good entente,   (295)
But thi werke harde is to parfourme, I drede.
Thi brain, par cas, therto not wole assente,
And wel thou woost it moot assente nede
Or thou aboute bringe suche a dede.
Nowe, in good feith, I rede as for thi best: (300)
That purpos caste oute of thi myndis chest.

'Thi besy studie aboute suche matere
Hath causid thee to stirte into the plite   leap
That thou were in, as fer as I can heere.
And though thou deme thou be therof quite,   (305)
Abide, and thi purpose putte in respite

Til that right wel stablischid be thi brain.
And therto thanne I wole assente fain.   gladly

'Though a stronge fir that was in an herthe late
Withdrawen be and swepte awey ful clene,   (310)
Yit aftirwarde bothe the herthe and plate
Ben of the fir warme, though no fir be sene
There as that it was. And right so I mene:
Although passid be the greet of thi seeknesse,   greatest part
Yit lurke in thee may sum of hir warmnesse.'   (315)

'O what is yow, freend, *Benedicite*?
Right nowe, whanne I yow redde my compleinte,
Made it not mynde it standith wel with me?
Myn herte with youre speche bigynneth to feinte.
Shullen we be nowe al newe to aqueinte   (320)
That han so wel aqueinted be ful yore?
What! han ye nowe lerned a newer lore?'

(323-364: Hoccleve attacks his friend's unfriendly scepticism,
saying that his attachment to the friend is absolute. He quotes
Cicero and Solomon in support of his strong views on friendship,
and he could quote other authorities. Then he continues:)

'But as I seide er (and soth it is)   (365)
My sclendre wit fele I as sad and stable   solid
As evere it was at any time or this,
Thanked be oure lorde ihesu merciable'.
'Yit, Thomas, herken a worde, and be suffrable   patient
And take not my speche in displesaunce.   (370)
In me shalt thow nowe finde no variaunce.

'I am thi frende, as that I have evere ben
And evere wole, doute it not at al.
But triste wel, it is but selden seen
That any wight that caught hath suche a fal   (375)
As thi seeknesse was, that aftir shal

39

Be of suche disposicioun and might
As he was erst; and so seith every wight.

'Of studie was engendrid thi seeknesse,
And that was harde. Woldest thou nowe agein   (380)
Entre into that laborus bisinesse?
Sithen it thi mynde and eke thi wit had slain,
Thi conceit is not worth a paindemain.   cake
Let be, let be: besie thee so no more
Leste thee repente and rewe it overe sore.   (385)

'My reede procedith not of frowarde wil,
But it is seide of verry frendlyhede.
For, if so causid seeknesse on me fil
As dide on thee, right evene as I thee rede
So wolde I do my silf, it is no drede.   (390)
And salomon bit aftir counsel do,
And good it is conforme thee therto.

'He that hath oones in suche plit yfalle,
But he wel rule him, may in slippe efte.
This rede I thee, for ought that may befalle: (395)
Sithen that seeknesse god hath the birefte,
The cause eschewe, for it is good lefte.
Namely, thing of thoughtful studie caughte
Perilous it is, as it hath me ben taughte.

'Right as a theef that hath escapid oones   (400)
The roop, no drede hath efte his art to use.
Til that the trees him weie up, body and boones,
So loth is him his sory crafte refuse.
So farest thou: joie hast thou for to muse
Uppon thi book and therynne stare and poure,   (405)
Til that it thi witt consume and devoure.

'I can no more; but that the later errour
Werse is, reede I, than that was beforn.

40

The smerte of studie ought be a mirrour
To thee. Lete yit thi studie be forborn.   (410)
Have of my wordis no disdein or scorn;
For that I seie, of frendly tendirnesse   what
I seie it al, as wisly god me blesse.

'If thee not list uppon thi silfe to rewe,
Thomas, who shal on the rewe, I the preie?   (415)
Nowe do forthe, let see, and thin harme rennewe,   if you continue
And hevyer shal it peise and weie
Than it dide er (therto my lyf I leie);
And that wolde overemoche the harme and greve.'
'Frende, as to that, answere I shal bileve.   quickly

'Whereas that ye demen of me and trowe   (421)
That I of studie my dissese took
(Wiche conceit eke amonge the peple is sowe),   opinion
Trustith right wel that nevere studie in book
Was cause why my mynde me forsook;   (425)
But it was causid of my longe seeknesse
And otherwise not, in sothfastnesse.

(428-490: Hoccleve bids the friend not to doubt him again, saying
he is determined to proceed. The friend agrees that Hoccleve's
reasoning-process seems sound, but he fears that the difficulty
of the new study may wear it out:)

'But as hertly as I can or may,
Sithen that thou wilte to that labour the dresse,
I preie the, by al manere way,
Thy wittis to conserve in her freisshenesse.
Whanne thou therto goost, take of it the lesse.   in moderation
To muse longe in an harde matere   (496)
The wit of man abieth it ful dere.'

'Freend, I not medle of materis greete.
Therto not strecche may myn intellecte.

41

I nevere yit was brent with studies hete.   (500)
Let no man holde me therynne suspecte.
If I not lightly may cacche the effecte
Of thing in wiche laboure I me purpose,
A deu, my studie! anoon my book I close.

'By stirtis, whanne that a fresshe lust me taketh,   starts
Wole I me bisie now and now a lite.   (506)
But whanne my lust dulleth and aslaketh,
I stinte wole and no lenger write.
And parde, frende, that may not hindre a mite,   harm
As that it semeth to my symple avis.   opinion
Jugeth youre silfe; ye bene prudent and wys.'   (511)

(512-693: the friend is now convinced and urges Hoccleve to
write what he wants. But he reminds Hoccleve that he told him
last September that he owed a book to the Lord Lieutenant,
Duke Humfrey of Gloucester. Hoccleve remembers and says that
this new book is meant for him, but he wonders what would
be most suitable. He thought of translating Vegetius' *On Chivalry*,
but the Duke knows everything about that, as his exploits at the
siege of Cherbourg and his victory at Constantine testify. All his
deeds, such as at the siege of Rouen, should be chronicled. What
can Hoccleve offer him? The friend suggests 'good mateer and
vertuous', and Hoccleve asks what? After reflection, the friend
suggests that, since it is Lent, Hoccleve should write in atonement
for the ill things he has written of women in the past. He must
write in praise of them because they hate dispraise. He quotes
his authority:)

'The wyf of Bathe take I for auctrice   authority
That wymmen han no joie ne deinte   liking
That men shulde uppon hem putte any vice.   (696)
I woot wel so, or like to that, seith she.
By wordis writen, Thomas, yelde the.
Even as thou by scripture hast hem offendid,
Right so lat it be by writiyng amendid.'   (700)

42

'Freend, though I do so, what lust or pleisir
Shal my lorde therynne have? Noon, thinkith me.'
'Yis, Thomas, yis. His lust and his desir
Is, as it wel sit to his hie degre,   befits
For his disporte and mirthe, in honeste   (705)
With ladies for to have daliaunce.
And this booke wole he hem shewe perchaunce.

'And sithen he thi good lorde is, he be may
For thee suche a meene that the lightlyere
Shullen thei forgeve the. Putte in assay   (710)
My counseil; let see. Not shal it thee dere.   harm
So wolde I do if in thi plite I were.
Leie hand on thi brest if thou wilt so do,
Or leve. I can no more seie therto.

'But though to wymmen thou thin herte bowe,   (715)
Axinge her graces with greet repentaunce
For thi giltees, thee wole I not alowe
To take on thee suche rule and governaunce
As thei thee reede wolde. For grevaunce
So greet ther folowe might of it, parcas,   (720)
That thou repente it shuldist evere, Thomas.

'Adam bigilid was thorugh Eves reed,
And siker so was she by the serpent
To whom god seide: "this womman thin heed
Breke shal, for thorugh thin enticement   (725)
She hath ybroke my commandement".
O sithen womman had on the fende suche might,
To breke a mannes heed it semeth light.

'For whi, let noon housbonde thinke it shame   therefore
Ne repreef unto hym ne vilenye   disgrace
That his wyf dooth to him that selve same.   (731)
Hir resoun axith to have of men the maistrie.
Though hooly writ witnesse it and testifie

43

Man shulde of hem have dominacioun,   (734)
It is the revers in probacioun.   *the proof*

'Hange up his hachet and sette him adoun!   *give up*
For womman wole assente in no manere
Unto that pointe ne that conclusioun.
Thomas, howe is it bitwixe the and thi fere?'   *comrade*
'Wel, wel,' quod I, 'what list you therof to here?   (740)
My wyf myg012t hoker have and greet disdein
If I shulde in suche caas pleie a solein.'   *behave sullenly*
      [i.e. complain

'Nowe, Thomas, if thou list to lyve in ese,
Prolle aftir wymmens benevolence.   *roam in search (prowl)*
Though it be daungerous, good is hem plese,   (745)
For hard is to renne in her offence.
What so thei seie, take al in pacience.   *whatever*
Bettir art thou not than thi fadris bifore
Han ben, Thomas. Be right wel ware thefore.'

'Freende, harde it is wymmen to greve, I graunte.   *dangerous*
But what have I agilte? For him that dide,   (751)
Not have I doon why, dar I me avaunte,
Oute of wymmens gracis slippe or slide.'
'Yis, Thomas, yis. In the epistle of Cupide
Thou hast of hem so largely said   *extensively*
That thei ben blak wrooth and ful yvel apaid.'   (756)

'Freend, douteles sumwhat is therin
That sowneth but right smal to her honour.   *tends*
But, as to that, nowe for youre fadir kyn
Considre I was therof noon auctour.   (760)
I nas in that caas but a reportour
Of folkes tales, and that thei seide I wroote.
I not affermed it on hem, god it woote.

'Whoso that shal reherse a mannes sawe,
As that he seith moot he seie and not varie;   (765)

For, and he do, he dooth agein the lawe
Of trouthe. He may tho wordis not contrarie.
Whoso that seith I am her adversarie
And dispreise her condiciouns and port
For that I made of hem suche report,   (770)

'He mysavisid is and eke to blame.   injudicious
Whanne I it spak, I spake compleiningly.   protesting their
I to hem thoughte no repreef ne shame.   [grievances
What worlde is this! Howe undirstande am I!
Looke in the same book what stiketh by.   (775)
Whoso loketh aright, therynne may thei see
That they me oughte have in greet chirtee,   affection

'And ellis woot I not what is what.
The book concludith for hem (it is no nay)
Vertuously, my good frende, dooth it nat?'   (780)
'Thomas, I not; for yit I nevere it say'.   saw
'No, freend?' 'No, Thomas.' Wel trowe I, in fay;
For had ye red it fully to the ende,
Ye wolde seie it is not as ye wende.'

'Thomas, howe so it be, do as I seide.   (785)
Sithen it displesith hem, amendis make.
If that somme of hem thee therof upbreide,
Thou shalt be besie ynow, I undirtake,
Thi kut to kepe. And nowe I thee bitake   hold your share: 'get
To god, for I moot nedis fro the wende.   [away with it'
The love and thanke of wymmen nowe god the seende!   (791)

'Amonge, I thenke thee for to visite   now and then
Or that thi book fully finisshid be,
For looth me were thou shuldist ought write
Wherthorugh thou mightest gete any mawgree.   ill-will
And for that cause I wole it overesee.   (796)
And, Thomas, nowe a dieu and fare weel!
Thou finde me shalt also trewe as steel.'   as

45

(Hoccleve follows with a dedication to ladies, swearing that he is their friend, and introduces his translation of the tale of the noble wife of the Emperor Jereslaus from the *Gesta Romanorum*.

At the end of this tale, the friend returns, and the following exchange acts as an introduction to the *Moralizacio* of the story. It is a striking example of the detachability of morals in late medieval writing, from Chaucer to Henryson's *Fables*.)

My freend, aftir, I trowe, a weke or two
That this tale endid was, hoom to me cam
And seide: 'Thomas, hast thou welny do?
To see thi werke I comen hider am.'
This tale I to him fette, and he it nam   took
Into his hand and he it oversy.   (6)
And aftirwarde he seide thus therby:

'Thomas, it is sumdel to my liking.
But is ther aught that thou purposist to seie
More on this tale?' 'Nay, my frend. Nothing.'   (10)
'Thomas, here is greet substaunce aweie.
Where is the moralizing, I the preie,
Bicome herof? Was ther noon in the book
Oute of the wiche that thou this tale took?'

'No, certis freend. Therynne was ther noon.'   (15)
'Sikerly, Thomas, therof I mervaile.
Hoom wole I walke and retourne anoon
(Not wole I spare for so smal travaile),
And looke in my book. There I shal not faile
To finde it. Of that tale it is parcel,   part
For I seen have it ofte and knowe it wel.'   (21)

He cam therwith and it unto me redde,
Levinge it with me, and home wente agein.
And to this moralizinge I me spedde,
In proose writing it, homely and plein,   (25)
For so counseillid he me to do certein.

And lo, in this wise and manere it seith,
Wiche to that tale is good be knytte, in feith.

(And the prose *moralizacio* of the story follows.)

LA MALE REGLE DE T. HOCCLEVE
Edited from Huntington Ms. 111. (formerly Phillips 8151)

O precious tresor inconparable!
O ground and roote of prosperitee!
O excellent richesse, commendable
Aboven alle that in eerthe be!
Who may susteene thyn adversitee? (5)
What wight may him avante of worldly welthe   boast
But if he fully stande in grace of thee,
Eerthely god, piler of lyf, thow helthe?

Whil thy power and excellent vigour
(As was plesant unto thy worthynesse) (10)
Regned in me and was my governour,
Than was I wel: tho felte I no duresse:
Tho farsid was I with hertes gladnesse;   stuffed
And now my body empty is, and bare
Of joie, and ful of seekly hevynesse, (15)
Al poore of ese and ryche of evel fare.

If that thy favour twynne from a wight,   part with
Smal is his ese and greet is his grevance.
Thy love is lyf, thyn hate sleeth doun right.
Who may compleyne thy disseverance (20)
Bettre than I, that of myn ignorance
Unto seeknesse am knyt, thy mortel fo.
Now can I knowe feeste fro penaunce,
And whil I was with thee kowde I nat so.

47

My grief and bisy smert cotidian   daily
So me labouren and tormenten sore   (26)
That what thow art now wel remembre I can
And what fruyt is in keepynge of thy lore.
Had I thy power knowen or this yore,
As now thy fo conpellith me to knowe,   (30)
Nat sholde his lym han cleved to my gore   got under my
For al his aart, ne han me nroght thus lowe.   [skirt

But I have herd men seye longe ago:
'Prosperitee is blynd and see ne may';
And verifie I can wel it is so   (35)
For I my self put have it in assay.
Whan I was weel kowde I considere it? Nay,
But what me longed aftir novelrie,
As yeeres yonge yernen day by day,
And now my smert accusith my folie.   (40)

Myn unwar yowthe kneew nat what it wroghte.
This woot I wel, whan fro thee twynned shee.   departed
But of hire ignorance hir self shee soghte
And kneew nat that shee dwellyng was with thee.
For to a wight were it greet nycetee   (45)
His lord or freend wityngly for toffende,
Lest that the weighte of his adversitee
The fool oppresse and make of him an ende.

From hennes foorth wole I do reverence
Unto thy name and holde of thee in cheef,   (50)
And werre make and sharp resistence
Ageyn thy fo and myn, that cruel theef
That undir foote me halt in mescheef,
So thow me to thy grace reconcyle.
O now thyn help, thy socour and releef!   (55)
And I for ay misreule wole exyle.

But thy mercy excede myn offense,   if not
The keene assautes of thyn adversarie
Me wole oppresse with hir violence.
No wondir thogh thow be to me contrarie.   (60)
My lustes blynde han causid thee to varie
Fro me, thurgh my folie and inprudence.
Wherfore I, wrecche, curse may and warie   curse
The seed and fruyt of chyldly sapience.

As for the more paart, youthe is rebel   (65)
Unto reson and hatith hir doctryne,
Regnynge which, it may not stande wel   prevailing
With yowthe, as fer as wit can ymagyne.
O yowthe, allas, why wilt thow nat enclyne
And unto reuled resoun bowe thee?   (70)
Syn resoun is the verray, streighte lyne
That ledith folk unto felicitee.

Ful seelde is seen that yowthe takith heede
Of perils that been likly for to fall.
For, have he take a purpos, that moot neede   (75)
Been execut; no conseil wole he call.
His owne wit he deemeth best of all,
And foorth therwith he renneth brydillees,
As he that nat betwixt hony and gall
Can juge, ne the werre fro the pees.   (80)

All othir mennes wittes he despisith.
They answeren no thyng to his entente.
His rakil wit only to him souffysith.   rash
His hy presumpcioun nat list consente
To doon as that Salomon wroot and mente,   (85)
That redde men by conseil for to werke.
Now, youthe, now thow sore shalt repente
Thy lightles wittes dull, of reson derke.

My freendes seiden unto me ful ofte
My misreule me cause wolde a fit, (90)
And redden me, in esy wyse and softe,
A lyte and lyte to withdrawen it.
But that nat mighte synke into my wit,
So was the lust yrootid in myn herte.
And now I am so rype unto my pit, (95)
That scarsely I may it nat asterte. escape

Whoso cleer yen hath and can nat see,
Ful smal of ye availlith the office. function
Right so, syn reson yoven is to me
For to discerne a vertu from a vice, (100)
If I nat can with resoun me chevice succeed
But wilfully fro reson me withdrawe,
Thogh I of hire have no benefice
No wondir, ne no favour in hir lawe.

Reson me bad and redde as for the beste (105)
To ete and drynke in tyme attemprely. moderately
But wilful youthe nat obeie leste
Unto that reed ne sette nat therby.
I take have of hem bothe outrageously to excess
And out of tyme; nat two yeer or three, (110)
But twenti wyntir past continuelly
Excesse at borde hath leyd his knyf with me.

The custume of my repleet abstinence, only abstaining when full
My greedy mowth, receite of swich outrage, eating
And homdes two, as woot my negligence, (115)
Thus han me gyded and broght in servage
Of hire that werreieth every age: wars on
Seeknesse y meene, riotoures whippe,
Habundantly that paieth me my wage
So that me neithir daunce list ne skippe. (120)

The outward signe of Bachus and his lure,
That at his dore hangith day by day,

50

Excitith folke to taaste of his moisture
So often that man can nat wel seyn nay.
For me, I seye I was enclyned ay   (125)
Withouten daunger thidir for to hye me,
But if swich charge upon my bake lay
That I moot it forbere as for a tyme,

Or but I were nakidly bystad   placed
By force of the penylees maladie,   (130)
For thanne in herte kowde I nat be glad,
Ne lust had noon to Bachus' hows to hie.
Fy! Lak of coyn departith conpaignie,
And hevy purs, with herte liberal,
Qwenchith the thristy hete of hertes drie,   (135)
Wher chynchy herte hath therof but smal.   stingy

I dar nat telle how that the fresshe repeir
Of venus' femel lusty children deere
That so goodly, so shaply were and feir
And so plesant of port and of maneere,   (140)
And feede cowden al a world with cheere
And of atyr passyngly wel byseye,
At Poules heed me maden ofte appeere
To talk of mirthe and to disporte and pleye.

Ther was sweet wyn ynow thurghout the hous   (145)
And wafres thikke, for this conpaignie
That I spak of been sumwhat likerous   fond of choice of food
Where as they mowe a draght of wyn espie
Sweete, and in wirkynge hoot for the maistrie   to the highest
To warme a stomake with therof they dranke.   [degree
To suffre hem paie had been no courtesie: (151)
That charge I tooke to wynne love and thanke.

Of loves aart yit touchid I no deel.
I cowde nat, and eek it was no neede.
Had I a kus, I was content ful weel,

51

Bettre than I wolde han be with the deede.
Theron can I but smal, it is no dreede.
Whan that men speke of it in my presence,
For shame I wexe as reed as is the gleede.   ember
Now wole I torne ageyn to my sentence.   matter

Of him that hauntith taverne of custume,   (161)
At shorte wordes, the profyt is this:
In double wyse his bagge it shal consume   purse
And make his tonge speke of folk amis,
For in the cuppe seelden fownden is   (165)
That any wight his neigheburgh commendith.
Beholde and see what avantage is his
That god, his freend and eek him self offendith.

But oon avauntage in this cas I have.
I was so ferd with any man to fighte,   (170)
Cloos kepte I me; no man durste I deprave
But rownyngly; I spak no thyng on highte   in a whisper
(And yit my wil was good, if that I mighte
For lettynge of my manly cowardyse,   in the face of prevention by
That ay of strokes impressid (were) the wighte),   marked by; the
So that I durste medlen in no wyse.   [man in question

Wher was a gretter maister eeke than y   (177)
Or bet aqweyntid at Westmynstre yate,
Among the taverneres namely
And cookes whan I cam, eerly or late?   (180)
I pynchid nat at hem in myn acate   underpaid; purchases
But paied hem as that they axe wolde.
Wherfore I was the welcomere algate
And for 'a verray gentil man' yholde.

And if it happid on the Someres day   (185)
That I thus at the taverne hadde be,
Whan I departe sholde and go my way
Hoom to the privee seel, so wowed me   enticed

52

Hete and unlust and superfluitee
To walke unto the brigge and take a boot,   (190)
That nat durste I contrarie hem all three
But dide as that they stired me, god woot. .   prompted

And in the wyntir, for the way was deep,   covered with mud
Unto the brigge I dressid me also,
And ther the bootmen took upon me keep   (195)
For they my riot kneewen fern ago.
With hem I was itugged to and fro,
So wel was him that I with wolde fare,
For riot paieth largely everemo;
He styntith nevere til his purs be bare.   (200)

Othir than 'maistir' callid was I nevere
Among this meynee—in myn audience.
Me thoghte I was ymaad a man for evere.
So tikelid me that nyce reverence   pleased, ridiculous
That it me made largere of despense   (205)
Than that I thoghte han been. O flaterie,
The guyse of thy traiterous diligence
Is folke to mescheef haasten and to hie.

Al be it that my yeeres be but yonge,
Yit have I seen in folke of hy degree   (210)
How that the venym of faveles tonge   flattery's
Hath mortified hir prosperitee
And broght hem in so sharp adversitee
That it hir lyfe hath also throwe adoun.
And yit ther can no man in this contree   (215)
Unnethe eschue this confusioun.   hardly

Many a servant unto his lord seith
That al the worlld spekith of him honour
Whan the contrarie of that is sooth, in feith.
And lightly leeved is this losengeour.   believed; flatterer
His hony wordes, wrappid in errour,   (221)

53

Blyndly conceyved been, the more harm is.   received by the mind
O thow favele, of lesynges auctour,
Causist al day thy lord to fare amis!

Tho combreworldes clept been 'enchantours'   useless encumbrances
In bookes, as that I have, or this, red: (226)
That is to seye, sotil deceyvours
By whom the peple is misgyed and led
And with plesance so fostred and fed
That they forgete hem self and can nat feele   (230)
The soothe of the condicion in hem bred,
No more than hir wit were in hire heele.

Whoso that list in *The Book of Nature*
Of Beestes rede, therin he may see,
If he take heede unto the scripture,   (235)
Where it spekth of meermaides in the see,
How that so inly mirie syngith shee
That the shipman therwith fallith asleepe
And by hire aftir devoured is he.
From al swich song is good men hem to keepe.   (240)

Right so, the feyned wordes of plesance
Annoyen aftir, thogh they plese a tyme
To hem that been unwyse of governance.
Lordes, beeth waar! Let nat favel yow lyme!   trap
If that yee been envolupid in cryme,   enveloped
Yee may nat deeme men speke of yow weel.   (246)
Thogh favel peynte hir tale in prose or ryme,
Ful holsum is it truste hire nat a deel.

Holcote seith upon the booke also
Of sapience, as it can testifie,   (250)
Whan that Ulixes saillid to and fro
By meermaides, this was his policie:
Alle eres of men of his conpaignie
With wex he stoppe leet, for that they noght   had stopped

Hir song sholde heere, lest the armonye   (255)
Hem mighte unto swich deedly sleep han broght,

And bond him self unto the shippes mast.
Lo! thus hem alle saved his prudence.
The wys man is of peril sore agast.
O flaterie! O lurkyng pestilence!   (260)
If sum man dide his cure and diligence
To stoppe his eres fro thy poesie
And nat wolde herkne a word of thy sentence,
Unto his greef it were a remedie.

A nay! althogh thy tonge were ago,   (265)
Yit canst thow glose in contenance and cheere.   make flattering
Thow supportist with lookes everemo   [comment
Thy lordes wordes in eche mateere,
Althogh that they a myte be to deere.
And thus thy gyse is privee and appert   (270)
With word and looke, among our lordes heere
Preferred be, thogh ther be no dissert.

But whan the sobre, treewe and weel avysid
With sad visage his lord enfourmeth pleyn   solemn
How that his governance is despysid   (275)
Among the peple and seith him as they seyn,
As man treewe oghte unto his sovereyn,
Conseillynge him amende his governance,
The lordes herte swellith for desdeyn
And bit him voide blyve with meschance.   (280)

Men setten nat by trouthe now adayes.
Men love it nat; men wole it nat cherice.   cherish
And yit is trouthe best at alle assayes.
When that fals favel, soustenour of vice,
Nat wite shal how hire to chevyce,   succeed
Ful boldely shal trouthe hire heed up bere.   (286)
Lordes, lest favel yow fro wele tryce,   snatch
No lenger souffre hire nestlen in your ere.

Be as be may, no more of this as now,
But to my misreule wole I refeere.   (290)
Wheras I was at ese weel ynow
Or excesse unto me leef was and deere,
And or I kneew his ernestful maneere,
My purs of coyn had resonable wone.
But now therin can ther but scant appeere.   (295)
Excesse hath ny exyled hem echone.

The feend and excesse been convertible,   synonymous
As enditith to me my fantasie.   imagination
This is my skile, if it be admittible: reasoning
Excesse of mete and drynke is glotonye;   (300)
Glotonye awakith malencolie;
Malencolie engendrith werre and stryfe;
Stryf causith mortel hurt thurgh hir folie:
Thus may excesse reve a soule hir lyfe.

No force of al this! Go we now to wacche   keep vigil
By nyghtirtale, out of al mesure;   (306)
For, as in that, fynde kowde I no macche
In al the privee seel with me to endure.
And to the cuppe ay took I heede and cure
For that the drynke apalle sholde noght.   go flat
But whan the pot emptid was of moisture,   (311)
To wake aftirward cam nat in my thoght.

But whan the cuppe had thus my neede sped,
And sumdel more than necessitee,
With repleet spirit wente I to my bed   (315)
And bathid there in superfluitee.
But on the morn was wight of no degree
So looth as I to twynne fro my cowche,
By aght I woot. Abyde! Let me see!
Of two as looth, I am seur, kowde I towche.   (320)

I dar nat seyn Prentys and Arondel
Me countrefete and in swich wach go ny me.

But often they hir bed loven so wel
That of the day it drawith ny the pryme
Or they ryse up. Nat telle I can the tyme   (325)
Whan they to bedde goon, it is so late.
O helthe, lord, thow seest hem in that cryme,
And yit thee looth is with hem to debate!

And why I not. It sit nat unto me   befits
That mirour am of riot and excesse   (330)
To knowen of a goddes pryvetee.
But thus I ymagyne and thus I gesse:
Thow meeved art, of tendre gentillesse,
Hem to forbere, and wilt hem nat chastyse,
For they, in mirthe and vertuous gladnesse,   (335)
Lordes reconforten in sundry wyse.

But to my purpos: syn that my seeknesse,
As wel of purs as body, hath refreyned
Me fro taverne and othir wantonnesse,
Among an heep my name is now desteyned.   (340)
My grevous hurt ful litil is conpleyned,
But they the lake conpleyne of my despense.   spending
Allas that evere knyt I was and cheyned
To excesse, or him dide obedience!   (344)

Despenses large enhaunce a mannes loos   praise
Whil they endure; and whan they be forbore,   given up
His name is deed: man keepe hir mowthes cloos
As nat a peny had he spent tofore.
My thank is qweynt, my purs his stuf hath lore,   quenched
And my carkeis repleet with hevynesse.   (350)
Be waar, Hoccleve, I rede thee therfore,
And to a mene reule thow thee dresse.   moderate

Whoso, passynge mesure, desyrith,
As that witnessen olde clerkes wyse,
Him self encombrith often sythe and myrith.   bogs down

And forthy, let the mene thee souffyse.   (356)
If swich a conceit in thyn herte ryse
As thy profyt may hyndre or thy renoun,
If it were execut in any wyse,
With manly resoun thriste thow it doun.   (360)

Thy rentes annuel, as thow wel woost,
To scarse been greet costes to susteene.
And in thy cofre, pardee, is cold roost.
And of thy manuel labour, as I weene,
Thy lucre is swich that it unnethe is seene   (365)
Ne felt. Of giftes seye I eek the same.
And stele, for the guerdoun is so keene,   reward (i.e. penalty)
Ne darst thow nat, ne begge also for shame.

Than wolde it seeme that thow borwid haast
Mochil of that that thow haast thus dispent   (370)
In outrage and excesse and verray waast.
Avyse thee, for what thyng that is lent
Of verray right moot hoom ageyn be sent.
Thow therin haast no perpetuitee.
Thy dettes paie, lest that thow be shent,   ruined
And or that thow therto conpellid be.   (376)

Sum folk in this cas dreeden more offense
Of man, for wyly wrenches of the lawe,   cunning twists
Than he dooth eithir god or conscience,
For by hem two he settith nat an hawe.   (380)
If thy conceit be swich, thow it withdrawe,
I rede, and voide it clene out of thyn herte.
And first of god, and syn of man, have awe,
Lest that they bothe make thee to smerte.

Now lat this smert warnynge to thee be.   (385)
And if thow maist heereaftir be releeved
Of body and purs, so thow gye thee   behave
By wit that thow no more thus be greeved.

What riot is thow taastid haast and preeved.
The fyr, men seyn, he dreedith that is brent.   (390)
And if thow so do, thow art wel ymeeved.
Be now no lenger fool, by myn assent.

Ey! What is me, that to my self thus longe
Clappid have I? I trowe that I rave.
A nay! My poore purs and peynes stronge   (395)
Han artid me speke as I spoken have.   urged
Whoso him shapith mercy for to crave
His lesson moot recorde in sundry wyse.
And whil my breeth may in my body wave
To recorde it, unnethe I may souffyse.   barely

O god! O helthe! unto thyn ordenance,   (401)
Weeful lord, meekly submitte I me.   prosperous
I am contryt and of ful repentance
That evere I swymmed in swich nycetee   folly
As was displesaunt to thy deitee.   (405)
Now kythe on me thy mercy and thy grace.   display
It sit a god been of his grace free.   befits
Foryeve and nevere wole I eft trespace.

My body and purs been at ones seeke.
And for hem nothe I to thyn hy noblesse.   (410)
As humblely as that I can, byseeke
With herte unfeyned: reewe on our distresse;
Pitee have of myn harmful hevynesse;
Releeve the repentant in disese;
Despende on me a drope of thy largesse   (415)
Right in this wyse, if it thee lyke and plese.

Lo, lat my lord the Fourneval, I preye,
My noble lord that now is tresoreer,
From thyn hynesse have a tokne or tweye
To paie me that due is for this yeer   (420)
Of my yeerly ten pounds in theschequeer:

Nat but for michel terme that was last.
I dar nat speke a word of ferneyeer,   past years
So is my spirit symple and sore agast.

I kepte nat to be seen inportune   would not wish
In my pursuyte; I am ther to ful looth.   (426)
And yit that gyse ryf is and commune
Among the peple now, withouten ooth.
As the shamelees cravour wole, it gooth;   (429)
For estaat real can nat al day werne   refuse
But poore shamefast man ofte is wrroth: sorrowful
Wherfore for to crave moot I lerne.

The proverbe is: 'the doumb man no lond getith'.
Whoso nat spekith and with neede is bete
And, thurgh arghnesse, his owne self forgetith,   timidity
No wondir thogh an othir him forgete.   (436)
Neede hath no lawe, as that the clerkes trete,
And thus to crave artith me my neede.   urges
And right wole eeke that I me entremete,   justice; interpose
For that I axe is due, as god me speede.   (440)

And that that due is thy magnificence
Shameth to werne, as that I byleeve.   refuse
As I seide, reewe on myn inpotence,
That likly am to sterve yit or eeve
But if thow in this wyse me releeve.   (445)
By coyn I gete may swich medecyne
As may myn hurtes alle that me greeve
Exyle cleene, and voide me of pyne.

BALADE TO MY GRACIOUS LORD OF YORK
Edited from Ms. Huntington 111

Go, litil pamfilet, and streight thee dresse
Unto the noble, rootid gentillesse   established
Of the myghty Prince of famous honour,
My gracious lord of Yorke, to whos noblesse
Me recommande with hertes humblesse   (5)
As he that have his grace and his favour
Fownden alway, for which I am dettour
For him to preye; and so shal my symplesse
Hertily do unto my dethes hour.

Remembre his worthynesse, I charge thee,   remind
How ones at Londoun desired he   (10)
Of me that am his servant and shal ay,
To have of my balades swich plentee
As ther weren remeynynge unto me.
And for nat wole I to his wil seyn nay   because
But fulfulle it as ferfooth as I may,   (16)
Be thow an owtere of my nycetee,   expresser
For my good lordes lust and game and play.

My lord byseeke eeke in humble maneere
That he nat souffre thee for to appeere   (20)
In thonurable sighte or the presence
Of the noble princesse and lady deere,
My gracious lady, my good lordes feere,
The mirour of wommanly excellence.
Thy cheere is naght, ne haast noon eloquence   (25)
To moustre thee before hire yen cleere.
For myn honour were holsum thyn absence.

Yit ful fayn wolde I have a messageer
To recommande me with herte enteer
To hir benigne and humble wommanhede,   (30)
And at this tyme have I noon othir heer

But thee; and smal am I, for thee, the neer.   nearer (my objective)
And if thow do it nat, than shal that dede
Be left; and that nat kepte I, out of drede.   would not wish
My lord, nat I, shal have of thee poweer.   (35)
Axe him licence; upon him crie and grede.

Whan that thow hast thus doon, than aftirward
Byseeche thow tnat worthy Prince Edward,
That he thee leye apart, for what may tyde,
Lest thee beholde my maistir Picard.   (40)
I warne thee that it shal be ful hard
For thee and me to halte on any syde   make a mistake
But he espie us. Yit, no force; abyde!
Let him looke on. His herte is to me ward   towards me
So freendly that our shame wole he hyde.   (45)

If that I in my wrytynge foleye
(As I do ofte; I can it nat withseye),
Meetrynge amis, or speke unfittyngly,
Or nat by just peys my sentences weye,   weight
And nat to the ordre of endytynge obeye,   (50)
And my colours sette ofte sythe awry: literary figures
With al myn herte wole I buxumly,   humbly
It to amende and to correcte, him preye;
For undir his correccioun stande y.

Thow foul book, unto my lord seye also   (55)
That pryde is unto me so greet a fo
That the spectacle forbedith he me   spectacles
And hath ydoon of tyme yore ago.
And for my sighte blyve hastith me fro
And lakkith that that sholde his confort be,   (60)
No wondir thogh thow have no beautee.
Out upon pryde, causere of my wo!
My sighte is hurt thurgh hir adversitee.

Now ende I thus: the holy Trinitee
And our lady, the blissid mayden free,   (65)

62

My lord and lady have in governance
And graunte hem joie and hy prosperitee:
Nat to endure oonly two yeer or three
But a milioun. And if any plesance
Happe mighte, on my poore souffissance,   (70)
To his prowesse and hir benignitee,
My lyves joie it were and sustenance.
Cest tout

AD BEATAM VIRGINEM
Edited from Huntington Ms. 111

Modir of god and virgyne undeffouled,
O blisful queene, of queenes Emperice,
Preye for me that am in synne mowled   grown mouldy
To god thy sone, punysshere of vice,
That of his mercy, thogh that I be nyce   foolish
And negligent in keepyng of his lawe,   (6)
His hy mercy my soule unto him drawe.

Modir of mercy, wey of indulgence,
That of al vertu art superlatyfe,
Savere of us by thy benevolence,   (10)
Humble lady, mayde, modir and wyf,
Causere of pees, styntere of wo and stryfe,
My prayere unto thy sone presente,
Syn for my gilt I fully me repente.

Benigne confort of us wrecches alle,   (15)
Be at myn endyng whan that I shal deye.
O welle of pitee, unto thee I calle,
Ful of swetnesse; helpe me to weye   outweigh
Ageyn the feend that with his handes tweye
And his might plukke wole at the balance   (20)
To weye us doun; keepe us from his nusance.

And, for thow art ensaumple of chastitee
And of virgynes worsship and honour,
Among alle wommen blessid thow be.
Now speke and preye to our Sauveour   (25)
That he me sende swich grace and favour
That al the hete of brennyng leccherie
He qwenche in me, blessid maiden Marie.

O blessid lady, the cleer light of day,
Temple of our lord, and roote of al goodnesse,   (30)
That by prayere wypest cleene away
The filthes of our synful wikkidnesse,
Thyn hand foorth putte and helpe my distresse,
And fro temptacioun delivre me
Of wikkid thoght, thurgh thy benignitee,   (35)

So that the wil fulfild be of thy sone
And that of the holy goost he menlumyne.
Preye for us, as ay hath be thy wone.
Lady, alle swiche emprises been thyne.
Swich an advocatrice who can dyvyne   (40)
As thow (right noon!) our greeves to redresse.
In thy refuyt is al our sikirnesse.   refuge

Thow shapen art by goddes ordenance
Mene for us, flour of humilitee.   mediator
Ficche that, lady, in thy remembrance   make firm
Lest our fo, the feend, thurgh his sotiltee,   (46)
That in awayt lyth for to cacche me,
Me overcome with his treecherie.
Unto my soules helthe thow me gye.

Thow art the way of our Redempcioun,   (50)
For cryst of thee hath deyned for to take
Flessh and eeke blood, for this entencioun
Upon a crois to die for our sake.
His precious deeth made the feendes qwake

And cristen folke for to rejoisen evere. (55)
From his mercy helpe us we nat dissevere.

Tendrely remembre on the wo and peyne
That thow souffridist in his passioun,
What watir and blood out of thyn yen tweyne
For sorwe of him ran by this cheekes doun. (60)
And syn thow knowest that the enchesoun   reason
Of his deeth was for to save al mankynde,
Modir of mercy, that have in thy mynde.

Wel oghten we thee worsshipe and honore,
Paleys of Cryst, flour of virginitee, (65)
Syn upon thee was leid the charge and cure   responsibility
The lord to bere of hevene and eerthe and see
And alle thynges that therynne be.
Of hevenes kyng, thow art predestinat
To hele our soules of hir seek estat. (70)

Thy maiden's wombe, in which our lord lay,
Thy tetes whiche him yaf to sowke also
To our savynge be they blessid ay.
The birthe of Cryst our thraldom putte us fro.
Joie and honour be now and everemo (75)
To him and thee that unto libertee
Fro thraldom han us qwit, blessid be yee!

By thee, lady, ymakid is the pees
Betwixt angels and men, it is no doute.
Blessid be god that swich a modir chees. (80)
Thy gracious bountee spredith al aboute.
Thogh that oure hertes steerne been and stoute,
Thow to thy sone canst be swich a mene
That alle our giltes he foryeveth clene.

Paradys yates opned been by thee (85)
And broken been the yates eeke of helle.

By thee the world restored is pardee.
Of al vertu thow art the spryng and welle.
By thee al bountee, shortly for to telle,
In hevene and eerthe, by thyn ordenance   (90)
Parforned is, our soules sustenance.

Now syn thow art of swich auctoritee,
Lady pitous, virgyne wemmelees,   flawless
That oure lord god nat list to werne thee   refuse
Of thy requeste, I wot wel doutelees,   (95)
Than spare nat foorth thee to putte in prees
To preye for us, Crystes modir deere.
Benygnely wole he thyn axynge heere.

Apostle, and freend familier of Cryst,
And his ychosen virgyne, seint Jon,   (100)
Shynynge apostle and evangelyst
And best beloved among hem echon,
With our lady preye I thee to been oon,
That unto Cryst shal for us alle preye.
Do this for us, Crystes derlyng, I seye.   (105)

Marie and Jon, hevenly gemmes tweyne,
O lightes two shynynge in the presence
Of our lord god, now do your bysy peyne
To washe away our cloudeful offense
So that we mowen make resistence   (110)
Ageyn the feend and make him to bewaille
That your preyere may so moche availle.

Yee been tho two, I knowe verraily,
In which the fadir god gan edifie
By his sone oonlygeten specially   (115)
To him an hows. Wherfore I to yow crye:
Beeth leches of our synful maladie;
Preyeth to god, lord of misericorde,
Oure olde giltes that he nat recorde.

Be yee oure help and our proteccioun,   (120)
Syn, for meryt of your virginitee,
The privilege of his dileccioun   special status, love
In yow confermed god upon a tree
Hangyng. And unto oon of yow seide he
Right in this wyse, as I reherce can: (125)
'Beholde heere, lo thy sone, womman',

And to that othir, 'heer thy modir lo!'.
Than preye I thee, that for the greet swetnesse
Of the hy love that god twixt yow two
With his mowth made, and of his noblesse   (130)
Conjoyned hath yow thurgh his blisfulnesse
As modir and sone, helpe us in our neede,
And for our giltes make oure hertes bleede.

Unto yow tweyne I my soule commende,
Marie and John, for my sauvacioun.   (135)
Helpith me that I may my lyf amende.
Helpith now that the habitacioun
Of the holy goost, our recreacioun,
Be in myn herte now and everemore
And of my soule wasshe away the sore. Amen.   (140)

TO THE DUKE OF BEDFORD
Edited from Huntington Ms. 111

Unto the rial egles excellence
I, humble clerc, with al hertes humblesse
This book presente; and of your reverence
Byseeche I pardoun and foryevenesse
That of myn ignorance and lewdenesse   (5)
Nat have I write it in so goodly wyse
As that me oghte unto your worthynesse.
Myn yen hath custumed bysynesse   habitual
So daswed that I may no bet souffyse.   dazed

67

I dreede lest that my maistir Massy   (10)
That is of fructuous intelligence,
Whan he beholdith how unconnyngly
My book is metrid, how raw my sentence,   argument
How feeble eek been my colours, his prudence   literary figures
Shal sore encombrid been of my folie.   (15)
But yit truste I that his benevolence
Compleyne wole myn insipience
Secreetly, and what is mis rectifie.   amiss

Thow book, by licence of my lordes grace,
To thee speke I, and this I to thee seye: (20)
I charge thee go shewe thow thy face
Beforn my seid maistir, and to him preye
On my behalve that he peise and weye
What myn entente is that I speke in thee.
For rethorik hath hid fro me the keye   (25)
Of his tresor: nat deyneth hir nobleye
Dele with noon so ignorant as me.

Cest tout.

BALADE AND ROWNDEL TO SOMER
Edited from Huntington Ms. 111

Cestes Balade & chanceon ensuyants feurent faites a mon Meistre,
H Somer, quant il estoit Soughtresorer.

The sonne with his bemes of brightnesse
To man so kyndly is and norisshynge,
That, lakkyng it, day nere but dirknesse.
Today he yeveth his enlumynynge
And causith al fruyt for to wexe and sprynge.   (5)
Now, syn that sonne may so moche availle
And moost with Somer is his sojournynge,
That sesoun bonteuous we wole assaille.

68

Glad cheerid Somer, to your governaille
And grace we submitte al our willynge.   (10)
To whom yee freendly been, he may nat faille
But he shal have his resonable axynge.
Aftir your good lust, be the sesonynge
Of our fruytes this last mighelmesse,
The tyme of yeer was of our seed ynnynge,   harvesting
The lak of which is our greet hevynesse.   (16)

We truste upon your freendly gentillesse
Yee wole us helpe and been our supportaille.
Now yeve us cause ageyn this cristemesse
For to be glad. O lord, whethir ous taille   tally (i.e.finances)
Shal soone make us with our shippes saille   (21)
To port salut? If yow list, we may synge;
And elles moot us bothe mourne and waille
Til your favour us sende releevynge.

We your servantes, Hoccleve and Baillay   (25)
Hethe and Offorde, yow byseeche and preye:
Haastith our hervest as soone as yee may.
For fere of stormes our wit is aweye.
Were our seed inned, wel we mighten pleye
And us desporte and synge and make game.   (30)
And yit this rowndel shul we synge and seye
In trust of yow and honour of your name:

ROWNDEL OR CHANCEON TO SOMER

Somer, that rypest mannes sustenance
With holsum hete of the sonnes warmnesse,
Al kynde of man thee holden is to blesse.

Ay thankid be thy freendly governance
And thy fressh looke of mirthe and of gladnesse.

69

Somer, that rypest mannes sustenance
With holsum hete of the sonnes warmnesse,
Al kynde of man thee holden is to blesse.

To hevy folke, of thee the remembraunce
Is salve, and oynement to hir seeknesse;   (10)
For why we thus shul synge in Cristemesse: therefore

Somer, that rypest mannes sustenance
With holsum hete of the sonnes warmnesse,
Al kynde of man thee holden is to blesse.

THREE ROUNDELS
*Edited from Huntington Ms. 744, formerly Ashburnham 133,
briefly owned by Gollancz.*

   Cy ensuent trois chaunceons: lune conpleynante a la dame monoie;
   et lautre la response dele a cellui qui se conpleynt;
   et la tierce la commendacion de ma dame.

1. To Money
Wel may I pleyne on yow, Lady moneye,
That in the prison of your sharp scantnesse
Souffren me bathe in wo and hevynesse
And deynen nat of socour me purveye.

Whan that I baar of your prison the keye,   (5)
Kepte I yow streite? Nay, god to witnesse!   closely confined

Well may I pleyne on yow, Lady moneye,
That in the prison of your sharp scantnesse
Souffren me bathe in wo and hevynesse
And deynen nat of socour me purveye.   (10)

I leet yow out. O now, of your noblesse,
Seeth unto me. In your deffaute I deye.   lack

70

Well may I pleyne on yow, Lady moneye,
That in the prison of your sharp scantnesse
Souffren me bathe in wo and hevynesse   (15)
And deynen nat of socour me purveye.

Yee saillen al to fer. Retourne, I preye.
Conforteth me ageyn this Cristemesse.
Elles I moot in right a feynt gladnesse
Synge of yow thus and yow accuse and seye: (20)

Wel may I pleyne on yow, Lady moneye,
That in the prison of your sharp scantnesse
Souffren me bathe in wo and hevynesse
And deynen nat of socour me purveye.

2. La Response. (Money's Reply)
Hoccleve, I wole it to thee knowen be:
I, lady moneie, of the world goddesse
That have al thyng undir my buxumnesse,   command
Nat sette by thy pleynte risshes three.   (4)

Myn hy might haddest thow in no cheertee   mercy
Whyle I was in thy slipir sikirnesse.   unreliable

Hoccleve, I wole it to thee knowen be:
I, lady moneie, of the world goddesse
That have al thyng undir my buxumnesse,
Nat sette by thy pleynte risshes three.   (10)

At instance of thyn excessif largesse   because of
Becam I of my body delavee.   washed away (*Furnivall, p.xl*)

Hoccleve, I wole it to thee knowen be:
I, lady moneie, of the world goddesse
That have al thyng undir my buxumnesse,   (15)
Nat sette by thy pleynte risshes three.

And syn that lordes grete obeien me,
Sholde I me dreede of thy poore symplesse?
My golden heed akith for thy lewdnesse.
Go, poore wrecche; who settith aght by thee?   (20)

Hoccleve, I wole it to thee knowen be:
I, lady moneie, of the world goddesse
That have al thyng undir my buxumnesse,
Nat sette by thy pleynte risshes three.

3. (Hoccleve's Humorous Praise of His Lady)
Of my lady wel me rejoise I may:
Hir golden forheed is ful narw and smal;
Hir browes been lyk to dym reed coral;
And as the jeet hir yen glistren ay.

Hir bowgy cheekes been as softe as clay,   baggy
With large jowes and substancial.   (6)

Of my lady wel me rejoise I may:
Hir golden forheed is ful narw and smal;
Hir browes been lyk to dym reed coral;
And as the jeet hir yen glistren ay.   (10)

Hir nose a pentice is, that it ne shal   overhanging roof
Reyne in hir mowth thogh shee uprightes lay.

Of my lady wel me rejoise I may:
Hir golden forheed is ful narw and smal;
Hir browes been lyk to dym reed coral;   (15)
And as the jeet hir yen glistren ay.

Hir mowth is nothyng scant, with lippes gray;
Hir chin unnethe may be seen at al;
Hir comly body shape as a footbal,
And shee syngith ful lyk a papejay.   parrot

Of my lady wel me rejoise I may: (21)
Hir golden forheed is ful narw and smal;
Hir browes been lyk to dym reed coral;
And as the jeet hir yen glistren ay.

THE REGEMENT OF PRINCES
Edited, unless otherwise stated, from Huntington Ms. 135
(formerly Phillips 8980).

Musyng upon the restelesse besynesse
Wyche that this troubly worlde hath ay on honde,
That other thynge than fruyt of bytternes
Ne yeledyth naght, as I kan understonde,
Att Chestres yn, ryght faste by the stronde,   (5)
As I lay in my bedde apon a nyght,
Thought me byrefte of slepe the force and myght.   worry

And many a day and nyght that wykkyd hyne   fellow
Hadde beforn vexyd my pore goste
So grevously that of anguyssh and pyne   (10)
No rycher man was nower in no coste.
Thys darr I seyne: may no wyght make hys boste
That he wythe thoght was bet than I aqueyntyd,
For to the deth hit welny hathe me feyntyd.

Besyly in my mynde I gan revolve   (15)
The welthe unseure of every creature,   prosperity
Howe lyghtly that fortune hit can dissolve
Whan that hir lyste that hit no lengyr dure.
And of the brotylnesse of hyr nature   brittleness
My tremlyng hert so grete gastenesse hadde   (20)
That my spirites were of my lyfe sadde.   weary

Me fel to mynde how that, naght longe ago,
Fortune's stroke doun thryste estate rial
Into myschef; an I toke hede also

Of many an other lorde that hadde a fal.   (25)
In mene estate eke sykernysse at al   middle
Ne sawe y none. But I se at laste
Where seurete for to abyde hir caste.   purposed

In pore estate sche pyght her pavylon   pitched
To covere her fro the storme of descendyng,   (30)
For sche knewe no lower discencion
(Safe only dethe, fro wyche no wyght lyvynge
Defende hym may). And thus in my musynge
I destitute was of joye and gode hope,
And to myn ese no thyng cowde I grope.   (35)

For ryght as blyve ran hit in my thought: quickly
'Thoughe pore I be, yit sumwhat lese I may.'   lose
Than demyd I that seurtee wolde nought
Wythe me abyde; hit ys naght to hir paye
Ther to sojourne as sche descende may.   (40)
And thus, unsekyr of my smale lyflode,   way of life
Thought layde on me full many a hevy lode.

I thought eke: 'yf I into poverte crepe,
Than am I entryd into sykernesse.   stability
But suche suretee myght I ay wayle and wepe,   (45)
For povert bredyth noght bot hevynesse.
Allas, where ys this worldes stabylnesse?
Heer up, heer doun; here honour, here reprefe;
Now hole, now seke; nowe bounte, now myschef.'

And whan I hadde rollyd up and doun   (50)
Thes worldes stormy wawes in my mynde,   waves
I sye well povert was exclusion
Of all wellfare reygnyng in mankynde;
And howe in bokys thus I wryten fynde:
'The werst kynde of wrecchidnesse is   (55)
A man to have been welefull or this'.

'Alas,' thoght I, 'what sykernes is that,
To lyve ay seure of grefe and of nuisaunce?
What schall I do? Best is I stryfe nat   (59)
Agayne the pees of fortune's balaunce.   weight
For well I wote that her brotell constaunce   know; brittle
A wyght no whyle suffre can sojorne   allow to stay
In o plyght.' Thus naght wyste I howe to torne.

For whan a man wenyth stande moste constante,
Than is he next hys overthrowyng,   (65)
So flyttyng is sche and so variaunte.
Ther ys no tryste upon hyr fayr laughyng.
Aftyr gladde loke sche schapyth her to stynge.
I was adradde so of hyr gerynesse   changeability
That my lyfe was but a dedly gladnesse.   (70)

Thys ylke nyght, I walwed to and fro,   tossed
Sekyng reste. But certeynly sche
Apperyd not, for thoght, my cruel fo,
Hadde chased her and slepe awey fro me.
And for I scholde not alone be,   (75)
Agayne my luste Wache proferyd hys servyse,   wakefulness
And I amyttyd hym in hevy wyse.

So longe a nyght felte I never none,
As was that same to my jugement.
Whoso that thoughty is, is wo-bygan.   (80)
The thoghtful whyght ys vessel of turment;
Ther ys no grefe to hym equipollent.   of equal power
Sche graveth deppest of sekenesses all.   digs
Full wo is hym that in suche thought is falle.

What wyght that inly pensyff is, y trowe,   (85)
Hys most desyre is to be solitarie.
That this is sothe in my persone y knowe;
For ever, whill that fretyng adversarie
Myn hert made to him tributarie

75

In sowkyng of the fresschest of my blode,   (90)
To sorow soul me thought hit dyd me gode.   alone

For the nature of hevynesse ys this:
Iff hit abounde gretly in a wyght,
The plase eschewythe he wher as joye is,
For joie and he nought can acorde aryght.   (95)
As discordant as day is unto nyght
And honour is adversarie unto schame
Is hevynesse soo to joye and game.

Whan to the thoughtful whyght is tolde a tale,
He heryth hit as though he thennis were.   (100)
Hys hevy thoughtys hym so pluke and hale   pull
Hider and thider, and hym greve and dere,
That hys eres avayle hym not a pere.   pear
He understandythe nothyng what men say,
So ben hys wyttes forgone hem to play.   (105)

The smert of thought y be experiense
Knowe as well as any man dothe lyvynge.
Hys frosty swote and fyry hote fervence   sweat
And troubly dremes, drempte al in wakyng,
My masyd hede, sleples, han of konnynge   (110)
And wytte dispoyled, and so me bejapyd,
That aftyr dethe ful oftyn han I gapyd.   longed

Passe over whan thys stormy nyght was gon   until
And day gan at my wyndowe in prye,
I rose me up, for bote fonde I none   cure
In my unresty bedde lengyr to lye.   (116)
Into the felde I dressyd me in hye,   haste
And in my wo y hert-depe gan wade,
As he that was bareyn of thoughtys glade.

By that I walked hadde a certayn tyme   (120)
(Were hit an owre I not, or more or lesse),   don't know

76

A pore holde hore man cam walkyng by me
And seid: 'gode day, sir, and god yowe blesse.'
But I no worde; for my so sekely distresse
Forbade myn erys usen her office,   (125)
For wyche this hold man helde me lewde and nyse,   churlish and
                                                        [foolish

Tyll he toke hede to my drery chere
And to my dedly colour pale and whan.
Than thought he thus: 'thys man that I se here   (129)
Al wronge ys wrastyd, be ought I se kan.'   twisted
He stirt to me and seyde: 'slepyst thowe, man?   started
Awake!'; and gan me schake wondyr faste.
And wyth a syghe I answerd at laste,

'A, who is ther?' 'I,' quod this holde grey,
'Am here', and he me tolde the maner   (135)
How he spake to me, as he herde me sey.
'O man,' quod I, 'for cristes lofe dere,
Iff that thou wylte aught done at my preyer,
As go thy wey; talke to me no more.
Thy wordes all annoyen me ful sore.   (140)

'Voyde fro me; me lyste no companye.
Encrese not my grefe; y have ynowe.'
'My son, hast thou gode luste thy sorow drye,   end
And mayst relevyd be? What man art thou?   (144)
Wyrke aftyr me; hit schall be for thy prowe.   profit
Thou nart but yong, and hast but lytell sen;
And full selde is that yong folk wyse ben.

'Iff that the lyke to ben esyd well,
As suffre me with the to talke a whyle.
Art thou ought lettered?' 'Ye,' quod I, 'sum dele.'   (150)
'Blessyd be god! Than hope I, by seynt Gyle,
That god to the thy wytte schall reconsyle,
Wych that me thynketh is ferre fro the went
Thorugh the assante of thy grevous torment.   compliance

77

'Letteryd folke han grettyr discression   (155)
And bettyr conceyfe can a mannys sawe,
And rathyr woll applie to reson
An from folye sonner hem wythdrawe
Than he that neyther reson can ne law,   knows
Ne lernyd hath no maner letture.   (160)
Plukke up thyn hert. I hope I schall the cure.'

'Cure, gode man? Ye, thou art a fayre leche!
Cure thy self, that tremblest as thou gost,
For all thyn art wole endyn in thy speche.
Hyt lythe naught in thy power, poor goste,   (165)
To hele me. Thou art als seke almoste
As I. First on thy selffe kythe thyn art,   demonstrate
And if ought leve, lette me then han parte.

'Go forthe thy wey, I the pray, or be styll.
Thou doste me more annoye than that thou wenyste.   (170)
Thou art as full off clappe as ys a mylle.   noise
Thou dost no thyng but grevyst me and tenyste.   irritate
Gode man, thou wotyst bot lytyll what thou menyst.
In the lythe nat redresse my nuisaunce,
And yitte thou mayst be well-wyllyd, perchaunce.   (175)

'Hyt most ben a grettyr man of myght
Than that thou art, that schulde me releve.'
'What, son myn, thou felyst not aryght.
To herkyn me, what schall it harme or greve?'
'Petyr, good man, though we talke her to eve,   (180)
All ys in veyn. Thy myght may not atteyne
To hele me, suche ys my wofull peyne.'

'What that I may or can ne wostow nought.
Hardely, son, tell on how hit is.'
'Man, at a worde, hit is encombrus thought   (185)
That causyth me thus sorowe and fare amys.'
'Now, son, and yf ther no thyng be bot this,

                         78

Do as I schall the say, and thyn estate
Amende I schall, bot thou be obstinate

'And wylfully rebell and disobeye   (190)
And lyst not to my lore the conforme;
For in suche case, what schulde I speke or seye
Or in my best wyse the enforme?
If thow hit wayve and take anothyr fourme
Aftyr thy chyldyssche, myssreulede conceyt,   (195)
Thowe dost wnto thy selfe harme and deceyt.

'O thyng say I: yf thou go fereles   alone
Al solitarie, and counceyl lakke and rede
(As me thynkyth thy gyse ys doutles),   practice
 Thou lykly art to bere a dotyd hede.   (200)
While thou art soule, thought his wastyng sede
Sowyth in the, and that in grete foysoun;   plenty
And thou, redles, naught canst voyde hys poysoun.

'The boke sayth thus (I rede hit yore agon):
"Wo be to hym that lyst to ben allone;   (205)
For yf he falle, helpe ne hath he none
To ryse". This say I be thy persone.
I fonde the soule, and thy wyttys echone   alone
Ferre fro the fledde and disparplid ful wyde. scattered
Werefore hyt semyth the nedyth a gyde.   (210)

(211-399: the old man offers to be the guide, and asks if it is
poverty that afflicts Hoccleve. He must tell it out; in this way
beggars are relieved. Beware of thinking too much, which the
devil can use to lead the thinker into error, as happened recently
to John Badby who denied the Real Presence and was burned for
heresy at Smithfield [in 1410]. It is only Pride that makes men
think they can prove or disprove faith by reason. He hopes Hoccleve
is not inclined to pry into God's mysteries, and Hoccleve assures
him he is not. Then he asks if Hoccleve thinks any better of him
than when they met, and he is told 'sumdel'. The old man then
characterises Hoccleve's opinion of him.)

'I wote well, son, of me thus wolt thou thynke: (400)
"This olde dotyd gresyll holt hym wyse.   greybeard
He wenyth maken in myn hede to synke
Hys lowde clappe, of wyche sett I no pryse.
He is a nobyll prechour, att devys.   certainly
Grete noyse hath thurgh his chynned lyppes drye   cracked
Thys day oute paste, the devell in hys ye!"   (406)

'Bot though I olde and hore be, son myn,
And pore be my clothyng and aray,   .
And naght so wyde a goun have as is thyn,
So small ypynched, ne so fressche and gay: pleated
My rede, in hap, yit the profite may.   (411)
And lyghtly that thou demest for folye   easily
Is gretter wysdam than thou canste espye.

'Under an olde, pore habyt regneth ofte
Grete vertu, thoghe hit mostre poorely.   appear
And where as grete array ys apon loft,   (416)
Vice is bot selden hid; that well wote I.
Bot naght reporte, I prey the hertly,
That fressch aray I generally deprave:
The worthy men mowe hit well use and have.   (420)

'Bot thys me thynketh an abusion,
To sen on walke in gownes of scarlett
Twelve yerdys wyde, with pendaunt slevys down
Unto the grounde, and the furre therin sett
Amountyng unto twenti pound or bette.   (425)
And if he for hit payed have, he no gode
Hath left hym wherwyth for to by an hode.

'For, thoughe he jette forthe amonge the prees   swagger; crowd
And overloke every pore wyght,
His cofur and eke hys purs ben penyles.   (430)
He hath no more than he gothe in ryght.
For lande, rent or catell he may go lyght.

80

The weyght of hem schall not so mekill peise   weigh
As dothe his gown. Ys suche array to preyse?

'Nay sothely, sone, hit is all misse me thynketh   amiss
So pore a whyght his lorde to counterfete   (436)
In hys aray; in my conceyt hit stynkythe.
Certes to blame ben the lordes grete,
Iff that I durst seyn, that here men lete
Usurpe suche a lordly apparaylle.   (440)
Hyt is nat worthe, my chylde, wythouten fayle.

'Sum tyme, afer men myghten lordys knowe
By her array, from other folke. Bot nowe
A man schall studie and muse a longe trowe   (444)
Wyche ys wyche. O lordes, hit sytte to yowe   is fitting
Amende thys, for hit is for your prowe.   advantage
Iff twyxte yow and your men no difference
Be in aray, lesse ys your reverence.

'Also, there ys another newe gett,   affectation
A foule wast of clothe and excessife.   (450)
Ther gothe no lesse in a mannys typette
Than of brode clothe a yerde, by my lyfe.
Me thynkyth this a veray inductyfe
Unto stelthe. Ware hem of hempen lane,   hangman's rope
For stelthe ys medyd wyth a cheklow bane. choking death

'Late every lorde hys own men defende   forbid
Suche grete aray, and than, on my parell,   word
Thys lande wythin a whyle schall amende.
In goddys name, putt hyt in exile.
Hit is a synne outrageouse and vyle.   (460)
Lordes, if ye your astate and honour
Loven, flemyth this vicious errour.

'What ys a lorde withoute his meynye?   attendants
I put a cas, that his foes hym assayle

Sodenly in the strete: what helpe schall he,   (465)
Whoos sleeves so encomburos so syde trayle,   to such a length
Do to hys lorde? He may hym not avayle.
In such a cas he nys bot a womman.
He may not stande hym in stede of a man.   place

'Hys armes two han ryght ynoghe to done   (470)
(And sumwhat more) his slevys upp to holde.
The taylleres, trowe I, mote heraftyr sone
Shape in the felde; they schull not sprede and folde   cut cloth
On her borde, thoghe they never so feyn wolde,   table
The clothe that schall ben in a gown ywrought.   (475)
Take an hole clothe ys best, for lesse ys nought.

'The skynner unto the felde mote also.
Hys house in London ys to streyte and scars   narrow
To don hys crafte. Sumtyme hit was not so.
O lordes, yeve unto your men her pars   due part
That so done, and aquaynte hem bet with mars,   (481)
God of bataylle. He lovethe nonarraye
That hurtyth manhode at preef or assaye.'   combat

(484-595: Nowadays, the town is full of unpaid tailors and furriers.
It was not so in the past; John of Gaunt's clothes, for example,
were not too wide, and they became him well. Nowadays there is
no need of brushing the streets, because the long sleeves of
'penniless grooms' brush them perfectly well. People in narrow
clothes are despised and flatterers loved. But Hoccleve must not
despise the old man for his unfashionable dress, or for being old,
as the young do. The scriptures enjoin respect for age: 'whan
youthe is past, is age sesounable', and Hoccleve too will be old
one day and of this mind.)

'Youthe ful small reward hath to godenesse,   regard
And peryll dredyth he non, wote I well.
All hys devocion and holynesse
At taverne is, as for the most dele.   (599)

To Bacus signe and to the levesel   leafy bower
Hys youthe hym halyth. And whan hit hym happyth   draws
To chirche gon, of nycete he most clappyth.

'The cause why men oughten thyder gon
Naght conceyve can his wyld, steerysch hede
To folowen hit. Also, but ys hit none   good
To tell hit hym; for, thoghe men sowe sede   (606)
Of vertu in a yong man, hit is deed
As blyve. His rebell gost hit mortifieth.
All thyng sauf foly in a yonge man dyeth.

'Whan I was yonge, I was recheles,   (610)
Proude, nyce and ryatous for the maistrie,   in the highest degree
And, amonge other, conciencelees.
By that sett I naght the worthe of a flye.
And of hem hauntyd I the compaignye
That went on pylgrymage to taverne   (615)
Weche before unthrift beryth the lanterne.

'Ther offeryd I well more than my tythe
And wythhdrowe holy chyrche his duetee.
My frendys me conseiled oftyn sithe,
That I, with lownes and humilite,   (620)
To my curat go schulde and make his gre.   reconciliation
Bot strawe unto her rede! Wolde I not bowe
For ought they couden prayen or wowe.   plead

'Whan folke wele rewlyd dressed hem to bedde
In tyme due by rede of nature,   (625)
To the taverne quykly I me spedde
And played at dees wyll the nyght wolde endure.
Ther the former of every creature
Dismembryd y with othes grete, and rente
Lym fro lym, or that I thens wente.'   (630)

(631-798: The old man continues his description of his dissolute
youth, in terms similar to Hoccleve's in *The Male Regle*: he was

83

guilty of covetousness, cowardice, pride, lechery; he has defouled wives, maids and nuns, and he has had a heap of 'nyce gyrlys' as his retinue. He squandered his misgotten gains, until God cured him by setting him at 'grounde ebbe' in poverty. The friends who had crowded around him in his wealth now desert him, saying 'I wyste well allway that hym distrue wolde his fool largesse. I told hym so, and ever he seyd nay' (715-717). But his poverty has caused him to repent, like Job. Hoccleve apologises for being rude at first, explaining that it was through madness, not disrespect for age or poverty. The old man asks:)

'Sauf fyrst, or thow any further procede,
O thyng of the wyte wolde y, my sone: (800)
Where dwellyst thou?' 'Fadyr, wythouten drede,
In the office of the privey seall y wone.   live
And wryte ther is my custome and wone
Unto the seall, and have twenti yere
And four com estren, and that ys ner.'   (805)

'Now syker, sone, that ys a fayre tyme.
The token is gode of thy continuance.
Come hyder, good, and syt adown her by me,
For I mote rest a whyle; hyt ys penaunse.
To me thus longe walke hit dothe nuisance   (810)
Unto my croked, feeble lymes holde,
That ben so styff, unneth y may hem folde.'   hardly

Whan I was sette adown, as he me preyd,
'Telle on,' saide he, 'how ys it wyth the, how?'
And y began my tale and thus y seyde: (815)
'My liege lorde, the kynge wyche that ys nowe,
I fynde to me graciouse inowe.   very
God yelde hym, he hath for my longe servise
Guerdoned me in covenable wyse.   fitting

'In the eschequer, he of hys speciall grace   (820)
Hath to me graunted an annuite

84

Of twenti mark while I have lyves space.
Myght y ay payed ben of that dutee,
Hyt schuld stonde well ynowe wyth me.
But payement ys harde to gete a dayes,   nowadays
And that me put in many foule afrayes.   (826)

'Hyt gothe ful streyte and scharpe or y hit have.
If y seur were of hit be satified
Fro yer to yer, than, so god me save,
My depe yroted grefe were remedied   (830)
Soffisantly. But how y schall be gyed   placed
Heraftyr, whan that I no lengyr serve,
Thys hevyeth me so that I well ny sterve.

'For, syn that y now, in myn age greene
And beyng in court, with grete peyne unneth   hardly
Am payed, in elde and oute of court, y wene   (836)
My purs for that may ben a ferthyng schethe.   close-fitting purse
Lo, fader myn, this dulleth me to dethe.
Now god helpe all; for, but he me socoure,   (839)
My future yerys lyke ben to be soure.   are likely

'Servyse, y wote well, ys none herytage.   leads to no inheritance
Whan y am oute of court anothyr day,
As y mot whan apon me hastyth age   must
And that no lengyr y labour may,
Unto my pore cote—hit is no nay—   (845)
I mote me drawe and my fortune abyde,
And suffre storme aftyr the mery tyde.'

(849-980: The world has no regard for service, Hoccleve continues,
as can be seen from the neglect of the gentlemen who fought in
the French wars. Those who are now prosperous knights must be-
ware of the overturn which fortune may bring them. Returning
to the annuity, he says that it is only six marks, and he can't live
on that, even if it *is* paid. His life is two-thirds over, and he
cannot learn to economise, being used to comfortable living.

People who have never known wealth are all right; but how will he keep himself in comfort? He lists the ways of life that he is unsuited for:)

'Wyth plough can I not medle ne wyth harowe, (981)
Ne wọt nat what londe good ys for what corne.
And for to lade a cart or fyll a barowe   load
(To wyche y never used was to forne)   before
My bak unbuxum hath swych swynke forsworne.   not pliant
At instaunse off wryting, his uerryour,   pressure; enemy
That stoupyng hath hym spylt wyth hys labour.

'Many men, fader, wenyn that wrytyng
No travayll ys; thei holde it but a game.
Art hath no foo but swych folk unkonnyng. (990)
But whoso luste disporte hym in that same,   whoever
Late hym contynue and he schall fynde hyt grame.   cause of anger
Hyt ys well grettyr labour than hyt semeth.
The blynde man of colyres all wronge demeth.

'A wryter mote thre thynges to hym knytte, (995)
And in tho may be no disseveraunse:
Mynde, ye and hande: non may from othyr flytte
But in hem mot be joynt continuance.
The mynde all hooll, wythouten varyaunse,
On yee and hand awayte mote alwaye, (1000)
And they too eke on hym, it ys no nay.

'Whoso schall wryght may not holde a tale
Wyth hym ne hym, ne synge thys ne that.
But all hys wyttes hole, grete and smale,
Ther most apere and halden them therat. (1005)
And syn he speke may ne synge nat
But bothe two he nedes most forbere,
Hys labor to hym ys the alengre.   longer

'Thys artificers se y day be day
In the hottest of all theyr besynes (1010)

Talken and syng and make game and play,
And forthe her labour passeth wyth gladnesse.
But we labour in traveylous stylnesse.
We stope and stare uppon the schepys skynne,
And kepe most our songe and wordys wythyn.   (1015)

'Wryting also dothe grete annoye thre
Off wyche ful fewe folkys taken hede
Sauf we oure self, and thys, lo, they be:
Stomak ys oon, whom stoppyng, oute of drede,   without doubt
Annoyeth sore; and to oure bakkys nede   (1020)
Mot yt be grevous; an the thrydde, oure yen
Uppon the wyte mochell sorowe dryen.   suffer

'What man that twenti yere and more
In wrytyng hathe continuyd, as have y,
I dar well seyn it smerteth hym full sore   (1025)
In every veyn and place of hys body.
And yen most hyt grevyth, trwly,
Of any crafte that man can ymagyne.
Fader, in feyth, hit spylte hath weny myn.'

(1030-92: Hoccleve hopes he has not bored the old man and asks
for his forbearance and advice. The old man asks if Hoccleve has
told everything and, when Hoccleve says he has, he points out the
folly of fearing poverty; even if he were a pauper he should not
compound his misery by lamenting but should accept it as God's
will. Christ praised poverty and practised it. For men to want
riches is an abuse, as can be seen from the following:)

'The pore man slepith full sikyrly
On nyghtes, thou hys dore be naght shitte,   shut
Where as the ryche abed besyly   (1095)
Castyth and imagyneth in hys witte
That necessarie unto hym ys hit
Barres and lokkes stronge for to have
Hys good fro theves for to kepe and save.

87

'And whan the dede slepe fallyth atte laste   (1100)
On hym, he dremeth theves comyn yn
And on hys cofyrs knokke and ley on faste.
An sum of hem pyken wyth a sotyll gyn   contrivance
And up ys broken hasp, lok, bar and pyn.
And in the hande goth and the bagge oute takyth: (1105)
For sorow off wyche oute of hys slepe he wakyth,

'And up he rysyth, fote and hande tremblynge
As that assaylled hym the palsie,
And at a styrte, wythowten taryenge,
Unto hys cofer he dressyth hym in hye.   (1110)
Or he ther come, he is in poynt to dye.
He hyt undoth and openyth hit to se
If that hys fals goddys therin be.

'He dredyth fynde hyt as that he hath drempt.
Thys worldes power and ryche habundance   (1115)
Off drede of peryll never be exempt.
But in povert ys ay sycur constance.
Who holdeth hym content hath suffisaunce.
And, sone, be my rede thou schalt do so
And by desyre of good noght set a sloo.'   (1120)

(1121-1414: The old man cites ancient examples of men preferring
good name to wealth. But surely Hoccleve *could* live on six marks
a year? Not in his accustomed manner, Hoccleve replies; besides,
he has a wife. His wits by which he lives are declining with his
welfare. The old man repeats his insistence on the virtue of
poverty; some men are virtuous and yet poor, by God's will.
Returning to Hoccleve's circumstances, he notes that Hoccleve
has failed to find advancement in the church. But churchmen
are often corrupt anyway:)

'Adayes nowe, my sone, as men may see,   (1415)
O chirche unto a man may nat suffice,
But algate he mot han pluralite;

88

Ellys he can not lyven in no wyse.
Ententyfly he hepyth hys servise   eagerly
In court: hys labour ther schall not moule.   grow mouldy
But to hys cure lokyth he full foule.   duty in the parish

'Though that hys chauncell roofe be al totorne,   full of holes
And on the hye auter hyt reyne or snewe,   altar
He rekketh not. The cost may be forborn
Crystys hous to repayr or make newe.   (1425)
And though ther be full many a vicious hwe   ewe
Undyr hys cure, he takyth of hit no kepe.
He tellyth never how rusty ben hys schepe.

'The oynement of holy sermonyng
Hym lothe ys uppon hem for to dispende.   (1430)
Sum persone ys so thredbare off konnynge   parish-priest, learning
That he can nat though he hym wys pretende.
And he that can may not hys hert bende
Thertoo, but from hys cure he hym absentyth,   duty
And what theroff comyth greedylyche he hyndeth.   seizes

'Howe he dispendyth hit be as be may,   (1436)
For unto that am y nothynge pryvee.
But wel y wote, as nyce, frecche an gay   extravagant
Sum of hem ben as borell folkys be,   lay
And that unsyttyng ys to her degre.   unfitting
Hem owyth to be myrrours of sadnesse   ought; sobriety
And wayfe jolyte and wantonnesse.   put aside

'But natheles y wote well ther ageyn
That many off hem gye hem as hem ought,   behave
And ellys were it grete pyte certeyn.   (1445)
But what man woltowe be, for hym the bought?'
'Fader, y may nat chese. In wylle y was
Han ben a prest; now past am y the raas.'
'Than art thou, sone, a weddid man parcaas?'

'Ye sothely, fader myn, ryght so y am.   (1450)
Y gasyd longe fyrst and wayted fast
Aftyr sume benefyce. And whan non cam,
Be proces y me weddyd att laste.   in due course
And, god hyt wote, hit sore me agaste
To bynde me where y was at my large.   (1455)
But don hyt was; y toke on me the charge.'

'A, sone, y have espyed and now see:
Thys is the tow that thou speke off ryght now.'
'Now, by the rode, fader, soth seyn yee.'
'Ye, son myn, thou schalt do well ynowe.   (1460)
Whan endyd ys my tale, than schaltowe
Be put in suche a way as schall the plese
And to thyn hert do comfort and ese.

'So longe as thou, sone, in the pryvy seal
Dweld hast, and woldest fayn han ben avaunced   (1465)
Unto sum chirche or thys, I deme well   before
That god nat wolde have the enhanced
In no suche plyght. Y holde the well chanced.
God wote and knowyth every hyd entente.
He for thy best a wyff unto the sent.   (1470)

'Yff that thou haddest, per cas, ben a prest,
Thou woldyst have as wantonly the gyed
As dothe the nycest of hem that thou seeste.   most foolish
And god forbede thou the haddest tyed
Therto, but yf thyn hert myght han plyed   bent
For to observe hyt wele. Be glade and mery   (1476)
That thou art as thou art, god thanke and herye.   praise

'The ordres of presthode and of wedlok
Ben bothe vertuous, wythouten fable.
But understonde wel, the holy yok   (1480)
Off presthode ys, as hit ys resonable
That yt so be, the more commendable.

90

The lesse of hem of mede hath habundance.
Men have meryte aftyr her governance.   way of life

'But how ben thy felaws lokyd to   colleagues
At home? Ben they nat wel ybeneficied?'   (1486)
'Yis, fader, yis. Ther is on clept "Nemo";
He helpyth hem; by hym ben they cherysschyd.
Nere he, they porely were cheficed.   provided for
He hem avaunceth; he fully her frende ys.   (1490)
Sauf only hym, they have but few frendys.

'So many a man as they this many a yere
Have wryten for, fynde kan they non
So gentyl or of her astate so chere   concerned about
That ones lyste for hem to ryde or gone   (1495)
Ne for hem speke a worde; but dombe as ston
They standen where here speche hem myght avayle.
For suche folke ys unlusty to travayle.   undesirable

'But yff a wyght have a cause to sewe   make a legal application
To us, sum lordes man schall undertake   (1500)
To swe hyt oute, and that that ys us dwe   pay for the writ
For our labour hym deynyth us nat to take.
He seyth hys lorde to thanke us wole he make.
Hyt touchyth hym; it ys a man of his.   it is his business
Where the revers of that, god wote, sothe ys.   (1505)

'Hys lettre he takyth and forthe gothe hys way,
And byddyth us to douten us nothynge
Hys lorde schall thanken us anothyr day.
And yff we have to sewe to the kynge,
Hys lorde may ther have al hys axynge.   (1510)
We schull be sped, as fer as that our bylle
Wole specifie theffect of oure wylle.

'What schall we do? We dar non argument
Make ageyn hym, but fayre and well hym trete,

91

Lest he report amys and make us schent.   ruined
To have hys wylle we suffryn hym and lete.   (1516)
Hard is þe holde suspect wyth the grete.
Hys tale schall be levyd and nat ourys,
And that conclusion to us full soure ys.

'And whan the mater ys to ende ybrought   (1520)
Off the straunge for whom the swte hath be,   stranger
Than is he to the lorde knowyn ryght noght.
He is to hym as unknowen as we.
The lord nat wote off all thys sotelte,
Ne we ne dar let hym of hyt to knowe   (1525)
Lest oure compleynt our selven overthrowe.

'And where thys brybour hath no peny payed
In oure office, he seyth byhynd oure bak
He payed, y not what: thus ben we betrayed
And desclaundred and put in wyte and lake   blame
Ful gyltles. And eke by suche a knake   (1531)
The man for whom the swte ys ys desceyvyd.
He wenyth we han off hym gold resceyved.

(1534-1848: The old man agrees that this cheating of the clerks is
disgraceful. Turning to Hoccleve's marriage, Hoccleve explains
that he married for love, not lust. The practice of seeking sexual
gratification for its own sake is deplored, notably the use of
'provocatives to engender . . . lust' [1609]. Marriage for money is
a current abuse, as is the habit of betrothing children before they
are old enough to love. Englishmen should marry English women
known to them, not 'her makes unseen' [1668]. Adultery too is
a great evil, as is seen in the Biblical stories of Pharaoh and Sarah,
and David and Bathsheba. Returning to Hoccleve's poverty, since
no lord will help him, he is advised to turn to Prince Henry
whom Hoccleve knows.)
[Lines 1849-68, missing in the Huntington Ms., are taken from
Arch. Seld. 53]

92

'Compleine unto his excellent noblesse
As I have herde the unto me compleine.   (1850)
And, but he quenche thy greet hevynesse,
My tunge take and slitte in peces tweyne.
What, sone myne, for goddes dere peyne,
Endite in frensshe or latyn thy greef clere,
And for to write it wel do thy powere.   (1855)

'Of alle thre thou oughtest be wel lerned,
Syn thou so long in hem laboured haast.
Thou of the pryve seel art old iyeerid.'
'Yit, fader, of it ful smal is my taast.'
'Nowe, sone, than foule hast thou in waast   (1860)
Dispente thi tyme. And natheles I trowe
Thou canst do bet than thou wilte do me knowe.

'What shal I calle the? What is thi name?'
'Hoccleve, fader myn, men clepen me.'
'Hoccleve, sone?' 'Ywys, fader, that same.'   (1865)
'Sone, I have or this herde speke of thee.
Thou were aqueintid with Chaucer, parde
(God have his soule best of any wight!).
Sone, I wole holde the that I have hight.'

(1879-1953: The old man says that surely, even if he doesn't
know Latin and French, Hoccleve can write in English? He says
to write as best he can to Prince Henry, asking about the annuity.
If he can't get anything this year, the best thing is to write for
him 'a goodly tale or two'. He must be careful to avoid flattery
though; 'favel' will not get him anywhere with this prince. Great
lords need to have truth spoken to them, so Hoccleve must write
some worthy thing about the duties of princes.)
[Lines 1954-60 are from Selden; thereafter Huntington again.]

'With herte tremblinge as the leef of aspe,
Fader, sith ye me rede to do so,   (1955)
Of my simple conceit wol I the claspe

Undo and lete it at his large goo.
But welaweye, so is myn herte woo
That the honour of englissh tunge is ded
Of wich I wont was have counseil and reed.   (1960)

'O mayster dere and fader reverent,
My mayster Chaucer, flour of eloquence,
Mirrour of fructuous entendement,   fruitful understanding
O universyl fadyr in science!   knowledge
Alas, that thou thyn exellent prudence   (1965)
In thy bed mortell myghtest nat byquethe.
What ayled deth? Alas, why wolde he sle the?

'O dethe, thou didist nat harme synguler
In slawthyr of hym, but al thys land hit smertyth.
But natheles, yit hastow no power   (1970)
His name sle. His hye vertu astirteth
Unslayn fro the, wyche ay us lyfly hertyth,   heartens
Wyth bokes of his ornat endytynge
That is to all thys lande ellumynynge.

'Hastow nat eek my mayster Gower slayn,   (1975)
Whos vertu I am insufficient
For to discryve? Y wote wel in certeyn,
For to sleen al this world thou hast ment.
But syn oure lorde god was obedient
To the, in feyth y can no bettyr say.   (1980)
Hys creatures mosten the obeye.

'Fadyr, ye may laugh at my lewd speche
 If that thou lyst: y am nothyng fourmel.   eloquent
My yong connynge may no ferther reche.
My wytt ys also sliper as an ele.   (1985)
But, how I speke, algate y mene wele.'   however
'Sone, thou seyst wel anow, as me semeth.
I kan no more; so my conceyt demeth.

'Now fare wele, son; go home to thy mete
Hyt ys hye tyme; and so woll y to myn.   (1990)
And what y have sayde the nat forgete.
And swyche as that I am, sone, y am thyne.
Thow seest wele age hath put me to declyne
And povert hath me made of good all bare.
I may not but prey for thy welfare.'   (1995)

'What, fadyr, wolden ye thus sodenly
Depart fro me? Petyr, cryst forbede!
Ye schall go dyne wyth me, truly.'
'Sone, at a worde, I mote go fro the nede.'
'Nay, fader, nay!' 'Yis, sone, as god me spede.'   (2000)
'Now, fader, syn hit may no other tyde,
Almyghty god yow save, and be youre gyde,

'And graunt grace me that day to se
That y sumwhat may quyte your goodnesse.
But, good fader, whan and where schull we   (2005)
Efte sones mete?' 'Son, in sothfastnesse,
I every day here at Carmes messe,   the Carmelites'
Hit fayleth not aboute the oure of sewen.'
'Wele, fader, god betake I you of hevene.'

Recordyng in my mynd the lesson   (2010)
That he me yafe, I home to mete went.
And on the morow set y me adowne
And penne and ynke and parchement y hent
And to performe hys wylle and hys entent
I toke corage, and whyles hyt was hoot   (2015)
Unto my lorde the prynce thus y wrote.

(2017ff.: At the end of this long prologue about the meeting with
the old man, the *Regiment* itself begins with a dedication to Prince
Henry of Wales, the future Henry V. The poem proper is in 15
sections of advice to princes, headed as follows: 1: On the
Dignity of a King, 2164-91;   2: On keeping coronation oaths,

and on Truth, 2192-2464; 3: Justice, 2465-2772; 4: The Law, 2773-2996; 5: Pity (i.e. *pietas*), 2997-3311; 6: Mercy, 3312-3458; 7: Patience, 3459-3626; 8: Chastity, 3627-3899; 9: On the magnanimity of Kings, 3900-4004; 10: That a king must not delight in Riches, 4005-4123; 11: The Virtue of Generosity, and the Vice of Prodigality, 4124-4473; 12: Avarice, 4474-4746; 13: Prudence, 4747-4858; 14: The Wisdom of Taking Counsel, 4859-5019; 15: Peace, 5020-5439.)

In the dedication, Hoccleve says he will draw upon the *Secretum Secretorum* and Guido's *De Regimine Principum*. His intelligence falls short for this task:

Symple is my gost and scars my letture	
Unto your excellence for to wryte	
Myn inward love. And yit in adventure	chance
Wole y me put, thogh y can but lyte.	(2076)
My dere mayster (god hys sowle quyte)	
And fader, Chaucer, fayn wolde have me taught;	
But y was yonge, and leryd lytel or naught.	learned

Alas, my worthy maistyr honorable,	(2080)
Thys landys verray tresour and richesse,	
Deth, by thy deth, hath harme irreperable	
Unto us don. Her vengeable duresse	vengeful
Dispoiled hath thys londe of the swettnesse	
Of retoryke. For unto Tullius	(2085)
Was never man so leke among us.	like

Also, who was heyr into philosophie	
To aristotell in our tonge but thou?	
The steppes of vergyle in poesie	
Thou folowdest, men wote wel ynow.	(2090)
That combreworld that the, my mayster, slowe	troublemaker
Wold y slayn were. Deth was to hastyf	
To renne on the and reve the thy lyfe.	

Dethe hath but small consideracion
Unto the vertuous, y have espyed: (2095)
No more, as schewyth the probacioun,   proof
Than to a vicious maistir losel tryede.   proven scoundrel
Amonge an hepe, every man is maistried
Wyth her, as wele the poore as ys the ryche.
Lered and lewed eeke ben to her ylyche.   (2100)

Sche myght han taryed her vengeance awhile
Tyl that sum man had egal to the be.
Nay, let be that. Sche knew wele that thys yle
May never man forth brynge lyke to the.
And hir office nedes do mot sche.   (2105)
God bad her so, I truste as for the best.
O maister, maister, god thy soule rest!

In the course of Hoccleve's advice to the king to take advice
in all matters (section 14), in support of his assertion that meetings
of the council should not be held on Holy Days, he quotes Chaucer.
The mention of his name prompts another passage in praise of him,
as well as the portraits suggested by lines 4992-8, the most
famous of which is in the Harley Ms. 4866, edited by Furnivall
for EETS.
*[The passage is missing from Huntington 135 and is edited from
Arch. Seld. Supra 53.]*

The firste finder of oure faire langage   founder
Hath seide in caas semblable, and other moo,
So highly wel, that it is my dotage   madness
For to expresse or touche any of thoo.   (4981)
Allas, my fadir fro the worlde is goo:
My worthi maister Chaucer, I him mene.
Be ye advocat for hym, hevenes quene.

As thou wel knowest, o blissid virgine,   (4985)
With lovynge herte and highe devocioun
In thin honour he wrote ful manie a line.

O nowe thin help and thy promocioun!   help forward
To god thi sone make a mocioun
Howe he thy servaunt was, maiden marie,   (4990)
And lete his love floure and fructifie.

And though his lyf be queinte, the resamblaunce   quenched;
Of him hath in me so fresshe lyfnesse   [appearance
That, to putte other men in remembraunce
Of his persone, I have here his licnesse   (4995)
Do make: to this ende, in sothnesse,   had made
That thei that have of hym lost thought and mynde
By this peinture may agein hym finde.

The ymages that in chirches bene
Make folke thenke on god and his seintis   (5000)
Whanne tho ymages thei biholde and sene,
Wheras unsighte of hem causeth unstreintis
Of thoughtis good. Whanne a thing depeint is
Or entailed, if men of it take hede   carved
(Thoughte of the lickenesse), it wole in hem brede.   (5005)

Yit somme men holde opinioun and seie
That noon ymages shulde imaked be.
Thei erren foule and goon out of the weie.
Of trouthe han thei scante sensibilite.   perception
Passe overe that. Nowe, blessid trinite,   (5010)
Uppon my maistres soule mercy have.
For hym, lady, thy mercy eke I crave.

THE ENVOY

(This envoy of 24 lines appears at the end of most Mss.—although
it is absent from some, and 'To the Duke of Bedford' comes at the
end of Dugdale Ms. 45—as well as separately amongst the shorter
poems of Huntington Ms. 111. It is edited from that manuscript
here, but with line-references to the whole *Regement*.)

O litil booke, who yaf thee hardynesse   (5440)
Thy wordes to pronounce in the presence
Of kynges ympe and princes worthynesse,   scion
Syn thow al nakid art of eloquence?
And why approchist thow his excellence
Unclothid, sauf thy kirtil bare also?   (5445)
I am right seur his humble pacience
Thee yeveth hardynesse to do so.

But o thyng woot I wel: go wher thow go,
I am so pryvee unto thy sentence,   meaning
Thow haast and art and wilt been everemo   (5450)
To his hynesse of swich benevolence.
Though thow nat do him due reverence
In wordes, thy cheertee nat is the lesse.   good will
And if lust be to his magnificence,   if it please his majesty
Do by thy reed. His welthe it shal witnesse.   (5455)

Byseeche him, of his gracious noblesse
Thee holde excusid of thyn innocence
Of endytynge. And with hertes humblesse,
If any thyng thee passe of negligence,
Byseeche him of mercy and indulgence,   (5460)
And that, for thy good wil, he be nat fo
To thee, that al seist of loves fervence.
That knowith god whom no thyng is hid fro.

Cest tout.

Page 19: Hoccleve's *Complaint* is the first of the 'Series' poems (dated 1421-2 by Furnivall), which are linked together by the device of exchanges with a friend who first appears at the beginning of the *Dialogue*. The items in the Series are *The Complaint*, the *Dialogue*, the tale of Jereslaus' ('Gerelaus' in the Selden Ms.) wife, 'Lerne to Die', and the story of Jonathas and Fellicula, ending with a dedication to Lady Westmoreland. I have edited the extracts from the Ms. Arch Seld. Supra 53 in the Bodleian Library rather than Furnivall's Durham Cosin V III 9 (which Schulz believes to be the author's own: see Bibliography) because the *Complaint* and the first 252 lines of the *Dialogue*, most of which I have included, are missing from the Durham Ms. and supplied only in Stowe's not very good sixteenth-century transcript.

Preferred readings from Durham/Stowe (Selden in brackets):
126 (omitted 'he'); 127 my (me); 248 All (As); 326 the (be); 352 men (me); 378 Whereof (Wel therof); 403 grauntide (illegible); 412 For (And).

l.1: At the end of the line in the Durham Ms. appears the name 'W. Browne', the poet William Browne of Tavistock who translated Hoccleve's Jonathas in 1614 and says he would have liked to edit more. (See *The Shepherd's Pipe*, Eclogue 1; London, Muses Library, 1894, ed. G. Goodwin. Vol. 2, p.117.)

Page 23: ll.152-4: 'Though' must mean 'as though' (a sense not in the O.E.D.)

Page 32: The *Dialogue*: preferred readings from Durham/Stowe (Selden in brackets):
31 ne (me); 109 (extra 'it'); 406 it (omitted); 710 ('it' in Selden after 'putte'); 752 I (ye).

ll.727-8: Furnivall's footnote wonders why a man's head is easier to break than a snake's?

l.760: Hoccleve could strengthen his argument by pointing out that the original author was herself a woman. This omission might suggest that he didn't know.

ll.764-5: a principle (or excuse) familiar from *The Canterbury Tales* A 731-42 and the epilogue to the *Decameron*.

Page 47: the next five items are edited from Huntington Ms. 111 (from which 6 poems were edited by G. Mason in 1796). At the head there is a letter to the owner and a table of contents by Tyrwhitt, dated 4 April 1785, with a confirmatory note by Furnivall. The elegant hand of the manuscript (again believed by Schultz to be Hoccleve's own) often finishes words with a flourish on particular letters which Furnivall occasionally half expands with a squiggle: e.g. 'punysscher' (4) and 'stryf' (12) of *Ad Beatam Virginem*. I have ignored the flourish in words like 'of(e)', but expanded by an 'e' in words like 'punysschere' by analogy wirh other occurrences. The *Male Regle* is dated 1406 by Furnivall. See Bibliography for E.M. Thornley's excellent discussion of it.

Page 52: l.175: I have supplied 'were' to make syntactic sense of a long sentence which remains awkward, though the sense is clear enough.

Page 54: l.227: 'deceyvours' for Ms. 'deceyvous'.

ll.233-4: for one version of *The Dialogues of Creatures Moralised*, see R. Tuve, *Allegorical Imagery* (Princeton U.P. 1966), pp.4ff. For the mermaid in particular, see the illustration and discussion of 'De syrenella' (Tuve, p.19).

ll.249ff. for Robert Holcot, see Beryl Smalley, *English Friars and Antiquity in the Early Fourteenth Century*, chapter 7, pp. 133-202, (Blackwell, Oxford, 1960).

Page 55: l.265: 'A' for Furnivall's 'As' and Mason's 'Ah'.

Page 56: ll.300-4: for this kind of sequence, cf. medieval wheel of fortune poems (e.g. R. T. Davies, *Medieval English Lyrics*, no. 136, p. 240. Faber, 1963).

Page 58: l.368: cf. the parable of the unjust steward (Luke, 16,3).

l.380: I have followed Mason and Furnivall in supplying 'an'.

Page 61: *Balade to York*. Furnivall identifies this duke of York as the father of the future Edward IV (the prince Edward, therefore, of line 38). From the fact that the prince (born 1442) seems to be able to read, he dates the poem at about 1450 which he then offers as the earliest date for the poet's death, as had Mason. Schulz argues convincingly that it is the son of the previous duke that is mentioned and that the date of the poem is c.1414. This is important because nothing else is dated conjecturally nearly as late as 1450, and Schulz offers c.1430 for the poet's date of death.

Page 63: *Ad Beatam Virginem* included as an example of Hoccleve's somewhat uninspired religious poetry. G.G.Smith, in *The Transition Period*, suspects (no doubt rightly) that the poem was over-estimated in the belief that it was by Chaucer. It is the only poem of Hoccleve's that Lounsbury admired; significantly, he doubted his authorship.

Page 70: the roundels are edited from Huntington Ms. 744, the third manuscript that the earlier Furnivall and Schulz thought was Hoccleve's own.

Page 73: *The Regement* is edited mostly from Huntington Ms. 135, in spite of the difference in linguistic forms from the other mss. and the considerable lacunae, because it is for the most part a reliable, early manuscript. A few changes in spelling have been made because of minor eccentricities in the orthography:

1: in replacing initial *yogh* by 'y', I have changed such words as 'yyt' and 'yyf' to 'yit' and 'yif' because the former look odd in a way that the manuscript does not.

2: 'w' is replaced by 'wh', and vice-versa. to whichever form is normal in modern English or when the manuscript form is confusible with another modern word. Hence 'where' (47); 'were' (1489); 'well' (417); 'who' (991); 'we' (1511).

3: similarly, 'hys' is changed to 'is' for ease (e.g. 97, 98) and 'is' to 'his' (201).

Preferred readings from Furnivall or other Mss. (avoiding Furnivall's inventions), against HM 135. HM in brackets:

14 to (omitted); 15 B- (of 'Besyly' omitted); 81 vessel (vesselyel); 87 is (omitted); 140 annoyen (amoyen); 179 it (hym); 417 well (whell); 604 conceyve (cause); 607 deed (drede); 623 they (yey); 630 (extra 'w'); 810 to (the); thus (thys); 822 I (omitted); 835 with (wyche); 839 but (omitted); 982 wot nat (omitted); 989 thei (the); 1010 besynes (besynesynes); 1025 it smerteth (smertyng); 1416 may (omitted); 1428 how (oon); 1433 can (omitted); 1449 line missing in HM; 1452 non (men); 1458 is the tow (omitted); 1475 han (omitted); 1477 and (omitted); 1967 he (omitted); 1975 (extra 'thou' after 'hastow').

ll.22-4: if the poem was written in 1411-12, its usual

dating, the reference may well be to Henry IV's increasing ill-health.

Page 74:   ll.55-6: Boethius *Consolation of Philosophy* II, prose iv, 4
Dante *Inferno* V, 121-3; Chaucer *Troilus and Criseyde* III, 1625-8; etc.

Page 77:   l.136: 'sey' is 'sigh', perhaps, since Hoccleve has said
nothing yet.

Page 78:   ll.178ff.: from here on the exchanges are headed 'pater'
and 'filius', suggesting a confessional exchange as in Gower's *Confessio
Amantis*. This important point is obscured by referring to the old man
as 'the beggar' as most commentators have. He is probably a mendicant
priest.

Page 79:   l.201: 'is' expanded to 'his' to avoid misinterpretation.

Page 86:   ll.981-5: cf. Skeat's note to *Piers Plowman* C VI, 24 (vol.
2, p.62 in Skeat's 2-volume edition). Langland's back too was too
long and 'unbuxom'.

Page 93:   ll.1857-8: I have taken Furnivall's reading, supported by
Royal 17 D vi and Douce 158, against Selden's:—

Sithen thou so longe in hevy labour hast
Contynued to the prive seel art olde yered.

ll.1864-5:   'Hoccleve', the reading of Huntington, Douce and
Furnivall's Harley, is chosen against the 'Occleve' of Selden and Royal.

l.1867: 'Chaucer', the spelling of Huntington and Harley is chosen
against the 'Chaucers' of Selden and Royal.

Page 96:   l.2087: 'heyr' is 'heir', not 'higher' as Skeat explained it.
See W.H. Williams in *Modern Language Review* 4, 1909, pp.235-6.
(His references are to the stanza divisions in Wright's edition, not to
the lines of the poem.)

Page 99:   l.5445: 'also' (Huntington 111 and Selden) is preferred
for the rhyme to Harley's and Royal's 'allone'.

BIBLIOGRAPHY

EDITIONS

The Works, in two volumes by the Early English Texts Society:

The Minor Poems (Huntington Ms. 111, Huntington 744 and Durham
Univ. Ms. Cosin V 9), ed. F.J. Furnivall and I. Gollancz (1892,
1925; ES 61 and ES 73). Revised A. I. Doyle and Jerome Mitchell
1970.

The *Regement of Princes, and 14 of Hoccleve's Minor Poems*, ed. F.J.Furnivall (ES 72, 1897).

The *Regiment of Princes* (Ms. Royal 17 D vi), ed. Thomas Wright (Roxburghe Club, 1860)

ANTHOLOGIES CONTAINING SELECTIONS FROM HOCCLEVE

E. Arber, *An English Garner, ingatherings from our history and literature*, Vol. 4, Birmingham 1882; pp.54-71. (*The Epistle of Cupid*)

E. P. Hammond, *English Verse Between Chaucer and Surrey*. (Durham, North Carolina 1927, pp.53-76).

J. A. Burrow, *English Verse 1300-1500* (Longmans 1977), pp.265-80.

CRITICISM AND BACKGROUND INFORMATION

The introductions to Furnivall's 2 volumes in particular; also the preludes to the selections from Hoccleve in Hammond and Burrow.

H. S. Bennett, *Chaucer and the Fifteenth Century* (Oxford 1947); pp.146-50.

H.S. Bennett, *Six Medieval Men and Women* (Cambridge U.P. 1955); pp.69-99.

Jerome Mitchell,*Thomas Hoccleve: A Study in Early Fifteenth-century Poetic* (University of Illinois 1968)

Ian Robinson, *Chaucer's Prosody* (Cambridge U.P. 1971); pp.190-99.

Penelope B.R. Doob, *Nebuchadnezzar's Children: Conventions of Madness in Middle English Literature* (Yale U.P.1974); pp.208-231.

C.F.E. Spurgeon, *500 Years of Chaucer Criticism and Allusion* (Cambridge U.P.1925); Vol. 1, pp.49-159.

ARTICLES

B. P. Kurtz, 'The relation of Hoccleve's *Lerne to Dye* to its Source' PMLA XL (1925), pp.252-75.

H. C. Schulz, 'Thomas Hoccleve, Scribe' *Speculum* 12, (1937); pp.71-81.

Eva M. Thornley, 'The Middle English Penitential Lyric and Hoccleve's Autobiographical Poetry' (*Neuphilologische Mitteilungen* 68, [1967] ; pp.295-321).